MORE

LIFE

IN THE

GOAT LANE

MORE LIFE IN THE GOAT LANE

Tales From *The Kidding Pen*

by

Linda Fink

Illustrations by Barbara Millikan

Triple F Press • Oregon

Printed in the United States of America on recycled, acid-free paper

Published by Triple F Press,
23000 Grand Ronde Rd.,
Grand Ronde, OR 97347

ISBN 0-9657048-2-3

Library of Congress Control Number 00-090709

This book is dedicated to the goat folk who heard about my horse-back riding accident and banded together to help pay the medical bills. Their online auction brought in nearly $5,000. Out of the goodness of their hearts, they donated kid goats, semen, guardian dogs, goat milk soap, artwork, and many other items. The cards, letters, e-mails and phone calls from all across the country lifted my spirits and made me aware of how kind people are, especially those crazy, wonderful people who raise goats. I was and still am overwhelmed by it all. Thank you, friends. I hope you enjoy your book.

ACKNOWLEDGMENTS

Thanks to Jeff Klein, publisher and editor of *United Caprine News*, for giving me a place each month to rave on about goats. All the stories in this book are adapted from The Kidding Pen column in UCN. Also thanks to those who have written to praise my first book, *Life in the Goat Lane,* and ask when the sequel would be out. Thanks to you, there finally is one — a mere nine years later.

Thanks to Barb Millikan, my faithful illustrator and friend; Sue Henry, editor extraordinaire; and Johnny Fink, who is, in spite of what I write about him, a truly kind and supportive husband. Also thanks to all those people who appear in this book, some of whom even gave their permission.

Special thanks to the many people, especially goat folk, who have stood by me emotionally, financially, and every other way through my various disasters. I don't know all your names, since many of your donations were anonymous and your delightful e-mails lost in my computer's innards; but you are all wonderful. Especially wonderful are the ones who wrote "I love your column. It's the first thing I read when I get my paper."

TABLE OF CONTENTS

PART I: Things I Have Learned

Part II: Those Wonderful, Crazy Goats and Their Wonderful, Crazy People

Part III: Seasonal and Other Sagas

PART I

THINGS I HAVE LEARNED

THE ACCIDENT

Since this book is dedicated to all those wonderful, caring folks who came to my aid after my accident, I'm reprinting the story of that accident more or less as it appeared in my Kidding Pen column in the July, 1999, issue of United Caprine News.

There are many challenges to be faced when taking care of livestock. One is taking care of livestock when you can't. Having fallen off my horse on Friday, June 4, smashing my left shoulder blade, snapping my left clavicle, breaking four ribs and partially collapsing my left lung, I am going to be learning how to tend goats with half a working body. As soon as I can tend goats at all. Right now, Johnny is doing chores. But let me start at the beginning of the story, with the accident.

My advice is: don't have one. They hurt and cost a lot of money and disrupt lives.

It happened like this. Mr. Smith is my 4-year-old Morgan gelding and the love of my life. I often jump on him bareback, with just halter and rope, for the short ride down to the bamboo pasture where I take out old fences. Polly, my mare, follows us. On Friday, June 4, I did that with a slight difference. After riding down to the gate into the bamboo pasture, dismounting and opening the gate, I decided to herd the sheep in with us, so they could graze the overgrown grass with the horses while I worked. I remounted Mr. Smith from the huge burl at the base of an old maple and we went after the sheep.

Mr. Smith was marvelous. At the slightest touch of my leg, he turned to follow the meanderings of the sheep. What a good horse he was and how responsive! It didn't occur to me that he might be turning on his own, following the movements of the sheep.

As the sheep began running down the one steep hill in this rocky, bumpy, woodland-turned-pasture, Mr. Smith broke into a canter, staying to their left to keep them heading in the correct direction. I have a fuzzy memory of the sheep veering right, with Mr. Smith veering sharply right almost simultaneously to cut them off. Not having Mr. Smith's quick reaction time, I went hurtling through the air straight ahead, down the hill.

The doctor said I must have landed very hard on my left shoulder, since I compressed and shattered the left scapula (shoulder blade,) snapped the clavicle (collar bone) and broke four ribs, at least one of which poked a hole in my left lung.

Fortunately, I didn't know any of this at the time. All I knew was I hurt an extraordinary amount, couldn't move my left arm, couldn't breathe, and felt like passing out. Mr. Smith was at my side, leaning down to nuzzle me, standing very still. I climbed to my feet slowly and he stood with his head down — he knew I was in pain and he was very sorry. I kept telling him, "It's not your fault, Mr. Smith. It's not your fault. You're a good boy."

"I should go close the gate into the bamboo pasture," I thought. The bamboo pasture leads to my newly planted arboretum, which I don't want devoured by critters. That's why I let them in the bamboo pasture only when I'm working nearby.

But I couldn't close the gate with one arm and it seemed such a long way away anyhow. The gate would have to stay open.

I needed to get back to the house to call for help. It had at last occurred to me that this was not my usual fall-off-the-horse-and-climb-back-on stunt. Who knows how long it might be before anyone found me down there.

The most direct route went through a gate that needs two hands and feet to open. No way in hell could I do that. My only choice was to walk up the lane and somehow get over a stock panel gate, which just might be climbable, though not openable, one-armed.

I took the lead rope off Mr. Smith's halter and wrapped it around my left arm and neck. I held one end in my right hand to support my left arm. Slowly, I trudged up the lane.

Seeing he was no longer needed, Mr. Smith galloped through the open bamboo pasture gate with Polly close behind. The sheep had disappeared in a different direction.

Every step of the way to the house (Johnny told me later it was a quarter mile), I told myself "You can't pass out. You can't pass out." Gingerly, I crawled over the stock panel gate and slowly moved past the goat barn. The girls all ran out saying, "Maa, maa, are you bringing us treats? Why can't we go to the bamboo pasture and arboretum and eat trees? Scratch my ears, please?"

I trudged onward.

At the house, I called Johnny who was working at a nearby neighbor's. "I fell off my horse and got hurt. Can you come home?"

By the time Johnny arrived moments later, I had cautiously felt around and discovered that my collar bone was at a very odd angle. I told him to call 911. He said it would be faster if he drove me. I said, "No, I need an ambulance."

Just a week before, a friend had been thrown from her horse (she had the grace to be dramatically bucked off instead of just falling off, like I did), landed flat on her back and had her husband take her to the hospital in their car. The hospital staff chewed her out royally. She had a spinal injury and could have been paralyzed by climbing into a car. I didn't think I had a spinal injury, but the thought of jouncing all the way to the hospital without being somewhat immobilized was not a happy thought.

I think the wait for the ambulance seemed longer to Johnny than to me. He hates to see me in pain. I'm not crazy about it, but I was in a zone where time was on hold. Too bad the pain wasn't.

A raft of x-rays showed the damage which was, as the emergency room doctor said, "quite dramatic." My left lung was only slightly collapsed and the doc had high hopes it would heal and refill on its own within a day or two. The bone doctor said all my broken parts would heal by themselves, no surgery necessary (or possible). He rigged up various harnesses and slings to hold things together.

I dictated a list of instructions to Johnny for milking goats and doing chores. I asked him to get the horses out of the bamboo pasture and close the gate. I was sure I'd be home in a day.

That was the beginning of a week-long hospital ordeal of dashed hopes as my lung refused to cooperate, horrid reactions to pain meds, and other hilarious tales of hospital life. Well, I'm sure they'll be hilarious someday.

But it was also the beginning of an outpouring of extraordinary love and support and caring from friends, family, acquaintances, and especially, goat folk. Sometimes it takes a crisis before we realize how much love there is in the world.

I also now realize that if you're going to ride a cutting horse, you need, at the very least, a saddle. My dad suggested two velcro strips — one for my horse's back and one for my butt. A goat folk friend sent me a tube of super glue.

One week after the fall, I was home with a tube hanging out of my chest, draining fluid and air from my thorax to keep the lung from collapsing again. I was sure that by the time this account appeared in the July issue of UCN, the tube would be out and I would be nearly mended. Well, the tube was out but the mending took a little longer.

Since pain meds were impossible for me, I had a raft of relaxation and autohypnosis tapes. Although tough at first, the pain became, eventually, manageable. I was and still am grateful to all the wonderful goat folk for their caring . . . and their super glue.

ACCIDENT BENEFITS

By the next month, the pain was gone, my arm was usable, and I'd begun to see the silver lining. Here is the August, 1999, Kidding Pen column.

Now that it has been over a month since I tumbled from my horse, I am mostly recovered and can look back at the good that has come from my accident. Paramount, of course, is learning the amazing kindness and generosity of so many people. But there were other benefits . . . of a sort.

Four metal gates are one benefit. They replaced woven wire "Wyoming gates," as we call them. Wyoming gates are nothing but continuations of the fencing, with a wooden post at the closing end that must be fitted into wire loops at the bottom and top of another wooden post. These monstrosities are difficult enough to close when you have two good arms. With one arm, they're impossible.

I grew so frustrated at not being able to close gates after I'd opened them to move animals that Johnny bought four metal gates and put them up. I think he was tired of following me around closing what I'd opened. Even though I have use of my left arm now, it still lacks strength — and he would still be following me around if he hadn't installed these lovely, easy swinging, easy closing gates.

A few days after the gates were up, a teenaged, goat-keeping friend came over and said, "I wonder how long before we'll get decent gates on our farm."

"Just have an accident and get badly hurt so you can't close the wire gates anymore and your dad will get so tired of following you around closing them that he'll buy metal ones."

She looked at me and said, "That seems like a mighty painful — and expensive — way to get gates." She's right. However, if an accident happens, one may as well take advantage of the circumstance any way one can.

Another benefit of my accident is that Johnny knows the names of my goats, at least the milkers. He had to do the milking for over two weeks. I gave him a list of goats with names and descriptions and he checked them off as they came into the milk room.

When I started milking again, I could milk only a few goats before the arm started aching too badly. So Johnny helped. That made it more difficult to keep track of which goats had come in for milking and which had not.

"Have you milked Erica yet?" Johnny asked one morning, after I wore out.

"I don't have an Erica."

"What do you mean? She's on the sheet."

"I don't have an Erica."

"Well, I've been milking her for two weeks."

"What does she look like?"

"She's kind of Annie-colored only smaller."

Annie is black with brown ears. The only other black-with-brown-ears goat I could think of was Celia, who was pregnant and bigger than Annie. Johnny pointed to a goat waiting by the door.

"That's Lyric," I told him.

Apparently, "Lyric" sounded like "Erica" when I dictated the names to him in the emergency room. And this black-with-*white*-ears goat is still Erica to Johnny.

When I first came home from the hospital with a tube and bag dangling from my chest, I couldn't do much of anything. When a goat came up sick, I could only give

Johnny instructions. It was sort of fun, for a little while, to say "clean this pen" . . . "use this medication" . . . "give her a bucket of clean water" . . . . I'd never had the opportunity to stand around and give orders before.

However, the thrill didn't last long. Neither did the opportunity. The tube soon came out and I was back in the barn doing what I could.

Now I can do most anything, although bucking hay is still beyond me and my weak left arm. I don't mind the deprivation. We bought a small load of 140# alfalfa bales the other day, and nobody expected me to help unload. In pre-accident days, I'd be out there grunting and sweating with Johnny. This time, he hired someone else.

Another side benefit (that I will stretch as long as possible) is that nobody expects my house to be clean. They assume I'm unable to clean it. If they saw me shoveling out the barn, which I do daily, they might wonder why I can't shovel out the house, but people don't generally see me working in the barn. If they do, I don't let them in the house.

Of course, my house was never a model for Good Housekeeping so the accident has not really made a difference. But it's a fine excuse. When enough time has elapsed for people to forget I was ever injured, I will have to come up with a new alibi.

"Oh those darn goats. They must have got in here again. Look at the mess they made!"

How the goats came to pile dirty dishes in the sink will be harder to explain. It's odd how I am healed enough to trim goat feet and ride my horse (yes, I'm back in the saddle) but can't do the dishes. At least, Johnny thinks it's odd. Personally, I think it's just another delightful side effect of the accident.

A few months later, the accident ceased to be an excuse. I was back to bucking hay. I held out longer on the dishwashing, but finally had to give in. We were out of clean plates.

SCIATICA and
SENSITIVE GOATS

In early November of 1995, I had the first of a series of health disasters. (The horse accident was merely a continuation.) Back then, my goats came through for me when I needed them to. This is particularly astonishing when you realize they are Nubians, those supposedly high-strung, wacked-out, mouthy brats of the goat world.

Admittedly, my Nubians have at times acted high-strung, wacked-out and mouthy. Many times, in fact. But when it counted, they didn't.

It counted on Sunday, November 5, 1995. That was the day I collapsed on the milk stand and had to wait for Johnny to find me and get me back to the house.

It really started the previous Friday, when I sent my sciatic nerve into paroxysms of pain when I threw, twisting as I turned, a sack of feed into the back of the pickup. Ten sacks of feed, actually. I think it was sack number 7 that did me in. However, I kept throwing. There were, after all, three more to load. Then I drove home and went to bed. That night I did chores very slowly.

The next morning I was in even more pain and did chores even more slowly, crying the whole time. Saturday night Johnny helped with chores.

Sunday morning, after not sleeping yet again, I tried to do chores. I could neither sit nor stand to milk. So I knelt behind the goats on the milk stand. By stopping every few seconds to breathe into the pain and writhe about, I finished all but Celia.

Celia always came in last. She didn't like Finegan, our Maremma guardian dog pup who, naturally, adored her and tried to lick her all over. So she had to be caught and dragged into the milk room, even when Finegan was locked out. She didn't trust he'd stay locked out.

I minced my way through the milk room door and into the goat pen to find Celia. The does stood and stared at me. They knew something was very, very wrong.

Did they flee as they usually do when they sense I'm late for an appointment and in a hurry? No. They stood perfectly still as I leaned my right hand on Winsome (big, fat, pregnant Winsome) then my left hand on Ember (big, fat pregnant Ember) then slowly extended my right hand to the back of Phantom (big and fat but not pregnant.) And so I made my way to Celia, who was standing in the rear of the herd, as always, eyeing me strangely.

Before I could reach for her collar, this doe who usually had to be run down and cornered, walked up and alongside me until I could rest my hand on her back. Slowly, Celia walked to the milk room with my weight leaning on her. Inside the milk room, she waited until I was holding on to the wall instead of her back, then jumped up and put her head through the hole without looking every which way for Finegan the way she usually did.

In fact, not one goat that morning moved one foot as I fumbled about trying to milk them without further irritating my screaming sciatic nerve. These are goats that had never before been milked from the rear and are not known for being highly cooperative. They are Nubians, after all.

It took me two hours to do 45 minutes worth of milking. Then I collapsed on the milk stand, unable to feed hay and unable to walk back to the house. That's where Johnny found me.

My saintly husband took over the chores. On November 8, I walked, with help, to the barn to say hi to the goats. Finegan flipped out, of course, and lavished me with kisses. The goats stood very quietly and, it seemed to me, sadly. No vigorous rubs on my legs or insistent nibbles or demanding cries.

I'm convinced that my goats knew I was in pain. Johnny said they were just being good because they were afraid that with him in charge, they'd all get sold if they weren't.

I think he's cynical.

Nine days after my milk stand collapsing act (which wasn't an act), I tried to help Johnny with chores. I milked from the rear again. Not one goat protested.

The does that came in from individual pens came straight in, which they did for Johnny also, but they went straight back out to their pens after milking, which they didn't do for Johnny and didn't for me before my back disaster.

Johnny was off feeding calves at the time. When he came back he asked if I'd had trouble getting Spirit and Awesome into their pens.

"No, they went right in."

He was amazed.

So was I. If I'd been in a hurry to go somewhere, Spirit would have run up and down the aisle six times before going into her pen, stepping on my feet with each pass. Instead, she walked sedately in front of me, stopping to wait for me to open the gate and let her in.

I think we should add sensitivity to the Nubian breed standard. Nubian: a large, proud, and graceful dairy goat of Oriental origin, known for high quality, high butterfat milk production and sensitivity to its owner's emotional and physical condition. Get impatient and your Nubians will do all they can to annoy you. Get hurt and they'll do all they can to help.

Or maybe sensitivity is a trait of all dairy goats, not just Nubians. It's just more obvious with Nubians because they're so obnoxious the rest of the time.

SURVIVAL INSTINCTS

When goats react in horror to a chair you've moved three inches in the milk room, I know it is because it could be a mountain lion. Goats are programmed to be leery of things that change. It's a survival instinct. I know this. But it still drives me crazy.

After I hurt my back, Johnny remodeled the milk stand to make it easier for me to sit and milk. He did a wonderful job. There are now seats on both sides of my two-goat milk stand, plus a foot-wide divider down the middle so the goats can't swing their rear ends away from me. It makes everything easier — milking, hoof trimming, clipping, doctoring, even Artificial Insemination.

The only thing not easier at first was getting the miserable beasts onto the "new" stand. They were sure that this was a device designed for something evil — like butchering. Or else the divider in the middle was a mountain lion.

They may not have known exactly what was wrong, but they knew something was and nothing in the world was going to make them climb onto that stand. Certainly not a woman with a bad back. (Their sensitivity to my condition ended as soon as I could walk upright.)

I pleaded and cajoled, threatened and screamed. They rammed their heads against the exit door, trying to escape. So I did what I always do under trying circumstances: I cried. Then, gritting my teeth, I dragged each one bodily up there in spite of my aching back and stuffed their terrified heads through the same holes that they'd been putting their heads through for years.

They ate. "Oh! Grain! Why didn't you say so?"

The next time they came into the milk room, we went through the whole procedure again. Except for a few. A precious few goats had no fear, apparently, of mountain lions. I have considered changing my breeding program to breed only for fearless goats. After all, I have guardian dogs to keep the real mountain lions at bay.

When the goats were all accustomed to the "new" milk stand, I made the mistake of putting my coat on the chair instead of over the towel bar. The suspicious goats knew my coat was a predator, perched on the chair waiting to pounce. I moved the coat. They do not consider it a predator when it's on the towel bar.

Which just goes to show why predators often sit in one place a long time watching their prey before they attack. If they stay there long enough, the prey will be convinced they belong and will wander up to them. I don't know how many predators are willing to sit in the same spot for three days, though, until my goats get used to them.

Horses are just as leery as goats. After all, they are also prey whose survival historically depended on eluding predators. But they come to trust their handlers and will do all sorts of fearsome things if their human says, "It's okay" even if it isn't. Not goats.

Goats figure they're responsible for their own survival and they are jolly well going to survive, no matter what fool thing their human says.

"It's okay?" they snort. "Give me a break. I know a change in scenery when I see one and a change in scenery means danger. So buzz off, lady, and let me out of here."

I have never found any way of convincing a doe except dragging her bodily past the "danger." Once the coat doesn't pounce or the milk stand doesn't behead her, she relaxes. Eventually.

Oh, sure, occasionally you can con a goat into doing

something against her better judgment if another goat does it first. But not always. There are followers and there are leaders. Most goats in my herd are leaders. They don't trust another goat to lead them safely any more than they trust me.

Celia was one of the goats who had no fear of the remodeled milk stand. I tried to get Phantom to follow Celia onto the stand. Instead, she stood in the doorway, looked at Celia, looked at the stand and snorted, "I always knew Celia was an idiot." Then she bolted for the far side of the barn.

Cha Cha's yearling daughter was also unafraid. Cha Cha and daughter were inseparable. But when Cherish jumped on the stand, her mother looked at her in horror as though to say, "Well, I did my best, but some kids you just can't teach." Then she planted her feet and refused all attempts to get her on the stand. Johnny had to help lift her.

We'd like to build a new barn someday. One thing holding me back is the thought of getting my herd accustomed to a new milk room. I'm not sure my back could take it.

THE VIRTUAL
GOAT SHOW

There's nothing like spring to make me notice goat udders. This is because I can finally find them. I dairy clip does before they freshen, thus uncovering what has been hidden for months, if not forever. It is exciting to uncover a first freshener udder. So exciting that I start thinking about showing again.

It's been years since I showed goats, thanks to various health and family crises plus plain ol' burn-out. But some of the udders appearing and reappearing on my farm each spring reawaken my long-dormant show fever.

When my energy level happens to be up a bit, and my sciatica gone, I harbor dangerous thoughts. "I think I could clip a few goats and take a small show string to a fair or two."

Not two days later, I somehow pull something in my left hip (it was the right one last time). I can still clean barns just fine; it's sitting that pains. In fact, after sitting for half an hour, I can barely stand up.

A few days after one hip episode, a rat trap caught my thumb. My entire thumbnail blackened and throbbed. Thankfully, I could still milk and type.

It seems that every time my body hears my mind talk about showing goats, it throws itself in front of a train, so to speak. The goats seem disbelieving as well.

One day not long after the rat trap incident, while

resting on my shovel, rubbing my hip and watching the goats munch hay from their feeder, the grunts and ear flicks and sideways glances between two old does seemed to hold more meaning than usual. I imagined the following conversation. (At least, I hope it was my imagination.)

"Can you believe she thinks she can do all the work involved in showing again? Why, the old bag can hardly walk."

"Yeah, and every time anyone so much as brushes against her fat thumb she screams. Hah! What a laugh. Can you imagine her doing all that clipping?"

"And bathing and packing the trailer and van and loading us and driving and unloading and setting up... Why, she'd collapse before she ever left the farm."

"And if she did get there, she'd probably take these young floozies with their high, tight udders instead of us. And they barely know how to be led much less how to pose in a show ring. She'd be dragged all over the place. What a joke!"

"Yeah, and these young things have never been off the farm. They'd freak out with all the noise and confusion at a fair. They'd probably jump out of their pens and she's too slow now to ever catch them."

"Hee, hee, can't you just picture it? Her yelling 'Stop that goat!' while she limps along holding her hip."

"If she *does* show, she should take us. We know what we're doing and she wouldn't have to do anything except walk beside us as we lead her to the show ring."

"Yeah, but she won't. Didn't you hear her tell that visitor the other day that my udder *used* to be high? Heck, wonder if she's looked at herself lately. She hasn't done such a great job of fighting gravity either. And *she* doesn't have the excuse of making milk year after year."

The does are probably right. Only in my dreams could I take twenty goats to a fair the way I used to. Or even five. But, now that I think about it, part of what I loved was planning which goats to take. I can still do that!

For a get of sire class I need three daughters of one

buck. I'll sort through all the goats and list who is from whom. Then I'll create virtual entries for produce of dam, get of sire, and dam and daughter. Why, this way, all my goats can be shown!

It won't matter if one doesn't make milk on the day of the show since there'll be no show. And if I don't get everyone clipped, so what? I can visualize.

The other thing I loved about fairs, of course, was talking to people. I could go goatless and talk; but, sigh, that's not the same as being part of the show.

In the past, when I didn't bring goats, I've worked as ring steward. That makes me feel more a part of things. However, due to one of my health problems (Meniere's Syndrome), I can't handle the barkdust in a ring. (Another reason that showing might be a bit difficult.)

Maybe I'll hold a virtual show here on the farm and invite my old goat-showing buddies to bring their photos. We can team judge the entries.

There will be no ribbons to buy or stalls to clean, no working the desk or hiring a judge. Heck, since we'll be using photos we don't even need to do it at the farm. We could meet at a restaurant and do our gabbing over lunch before bringing out the pictures.

Of course, the other thing I liked about fairs was premiums. A virtual show will have no premiums.

"And would it really be more difficult," I asked myself, "to take a few goats to a fair than to try to stand up after sitting in a chair for several hours judging a virtual show? I almost never have time to sit at a fair, so my hip might not be too bad a problem. And I could wear a gas mask to keep out the barkdust.

"As soon as my thumb heals," I decided, "I'll reassess the situation."

Then came the horse accident with broken shoulder blade, collar bone, ribs and punctured lung. A virtual show sounds better and better.

THIS IS RELAXING??

"Do you have to milk your goats every day?" non-farm friends ask, in the same tone of voice they'd use for "Does your husband beat you every day?"

"Yep. Twice a day," I tell them. "But I enjoy it."

In an attempt to prove that I'm not a masochist, I try to explain how wonderful it is to start and end each day nestled against warm goat sides. My friends then look at me with a combination of awe and abhorrence, the way you might look at a circus freak.

So I forge on, extolling the crisp, fresh morning air; the sweet smells of hay and of grain mixed with molasses; the warm nuzzles each doe gives me before she climbs off the stand. Before long, I have myself convinced.

That doesn't work with other goat owners. They know. I started to tell e-mail friend Sally Heeren, "Milking is a very relaxing time for me — a good beginning and ending to the day . . . "

Even through the computer and over the Internet, I knew I was treading on weak ground. Sally milks goats, too. So I tempered my enthusiasm with realism "...Except when somebody kicks over the bucket or steps on my foot or . . . "

Sally responded with her own dose of realism . . . "Or doesn't finish her feed so you stay awake all night worrying over what could be wrong and then she scarfs down her food and practically strangles herself to get to someone else's food the next morning.

"Or your husband picks just before bedtime to sing the old song about too many goats. Or just as you're dropping off to sleep he says, 'Oh yeah. Meant to tell you that black buck was off by himself hanging his head this evening when I passed the buck pen.'

"That will jerk you awake and send you to the buck pen in your nightgown and rubber boots to find him sleeping peacefully with his head on another buck but you just have to get him up and look him over and the other bucks get up and they all tell you how thrilled they are by this late night visit by rubbing all over you so after this false alarm you get to take another shower and hope you don't get it all off so the smell will wake up your husband who's snoring away without a care."

Nothing like a goat friend to bring you back to earth.

Or a year-old Holstein steer. Thanks to lousy cattle prices, I kept the steers longer than usual one year. The biggest one figured out that goat fencing was no match for him. In fact, I'm not sure he even noticed the fencing as he walked over and through woven wire and stock panels, leaving destruction in his wake.

Then came the late night I went to the barn for the calming routine of milking goats after a harried day visiting my sick mom in the hospital. I turned on the lights and was greeted by a deep "moo" from where I should have heard "baa". The big Holstein stood in the middle of the milker barn, taking up most of it, while the goats huddled in terror in a far corner.

I screamed and chased him. Or tried to. He was still a bottle baby, although a year old. I thought by keeping him on milk he'd be less apt to walk through fences looking for more feed. A 1000-pound, friendly, horned Holstein is impossible to chase. So I walked out of the barn and he followed.

The big oaf had mangled the stock panel gate getting in, but it was still latched so he couldn't get back out, naturally. After leading him through pouring rain and several gates to his pasture, trying to avoid the friendly rubs of his head and horns, and hoping I wouldn't lose my boots in the mud, I stomped into the house and hollered at Johnny. "That steer goes to the auction tomorrow! And I want fences fixed!"

I could get away with this screaming fit because Johnny knew I was stressed out from a week of hospital trauma with my mom. He called the auction yard the next morning. Fences began to be repaired that day. Milkings returned to tranquility.

Interspersed with hysteria, of course. That's how it is on the farm.

I will never convince some of my non-farm friends that milking a dozen goats every morning and night is peaceful and relaxing. The idea of trudging through rain and dark to squeeze teats simply does not appeal to a great number of people, without even considering the occasional excitement from wayward steers or sick goats.

THE CYCLE OF LIFE

I wrote this column shortly after my mother's death in March of 1997.

It is not possible to wallow in self-pity or sorrow when you live with animals. The day after my mom died in early March, I sadly walked to the barn to do chores for the first time in a week. Johnny had done the milking while I stayed with Mom at the hospital.

I was greeted by a doe about to kid. "Baa! Where have you been? Helpppp!!" Sonata is very vocal about her needs and not in the least interested in mine.

As it turned out, she did need help. The kid's tail was coming first. Alas, the placenta had already detached and the doeling was born dead. Sonata gave me a dirty look.

Luckily, there were more to come. Sonata soon spit out two more doelings from another placenta, apparently, since both kids were alive and healthy. Well, both were alive and one was healthy. The other was tiny and too weak to stand for the first twelve hours or so. I took it into the house, warmed it up, and fed it.

Since my brother's family was arriving very late that night for Mom's memorial service, I left a note on the table warning them that the kid goat in the box next to the woodstove would probably squawk when they came in, but it was okay. My non-farm brother and his wife and two young-adult children did not, unfortunately, read the note before the goat's sudden noise scared the socks off them.

"What a sick joke," said my niece. "Aunt Linda left a rooster in the house." After she saw that it was a cute baby goat instead of a rooster, she forgave me.

The next morning I put the kid back with Sonata — who would have nothing to do with it. She had decided that one kid was enough.

After a few choice words between us and a solid grip, Sonata stood while her littlest kid nursed. For two weeks I held (and threatened) Sonata while her diminutive doeling nursed. Eventually, Sonata gave in.

The day after the kidding mess, a yearling ewe, who was evidently not emotionally prepared to become a mother, dropped a dead lamb and a live lamb. I tried to convince her the live lamb was hers, but remaining unconvinced, she jumped out of the pen, and fled. So I heated up goat milk and let my city-bred niece feed the perky little motherless lamb while I called the friend who buys my bummers. She came an hour later.

"There's an awful lot of birthing and dying around here," observed my niece, as my friend drove off with the lamb. But Melissa gamely kept helping with chores.

The animals, I foolishly thought, will give me some time now to grieve my loss and commune with my relatives.

Wrong.

The day after Mom's memorial service another ewe lambed — this time in the far pasture. I'd moved the sheep onto new grass so I wouldn't have to feed them hay. I thought they were all through lambing. I didn't realize that little yearling was pregnant. Her lamb did not survive. I moved the sheep in closer.

A few days later my father left a message on my phone: "I'm bringing a calf that needs a mother."

Through my mom's final illness and hospitalization, Dad's Polled Herefords had been giving birth at the most inopportune moments. A neighboring rancher tended to them. When Dad took over the chores again, his cattle conspired to keep him as busy as my goats and sheep were keeping me.

The cow that calved the day my mom died went down a week later. That was the calf Dad brought to me. It quite happily drank goat's milk.

I don't mind bottle-feeding a baby that has lost its

mother. I just resent feeding babies whose mothers are perfectly capable of tending to them, but unwilling.

Not that my sheep or goats give a fig what I think. They go on birthing and dying and nurturing or not, no matter what my opinion. If anyone were to bother to ask me, I'd tell them I think it's time for the cycle of life to slow down a bit. It's been on fast forward around here long enough.

My niece and nephew, who had never before seen any creature arrive on earth, witnessed several comings . . . and goings . . . during their short visit. My nephew was overwhelmed by it all, but my niece, who is a farm girl at heart, said, "Hey, no big deal. I've lived in L.A. At least nobody's being murdered."

Although there are times I'd like to ship all the goats off to the nearest auction yard, when I nestle my cheek into a warm baby goat I know that the cycle of life is as wonderful as it is awful; that death is as necessary as birth.

But I wouldn't mind if my animals would give me a chance to catch my breath and drink in this new wisdom they're bound and determined to give me.

GOAT TROUBLE

Goats can cause trouble without even trying. One bit of trouble they're good at is sticking their heads where they shouldn't, and then being unable to unstick them. Especially if they have horns. But even without horns, heads get stuck in the oddest places.

Not infrequently, one or another of my bucks shoves his knobby head through the wooden boards of the corner hay feeders in the buck pens. There is no reason for a buck to try to get his head through those cracks. All the hay can easily be pulled out. But you can't convince a buck of that.

There is also no way he can get his head in there since the cracks are very narrow. Now and then, though, someone does it anyway. He rubs on a board enough to push it forward or back so his head fits, barely, between the slats. Of course, he can't pull it back out. I can't get his head out either, so I have to remove the boards with a hammer.

Bucks that repeatedly get stuck are bucks that get sold. I can put up with only so much stupidity. What if he were to pass on his proclivity for putting his head where he shouldn't? His daughters would spend all their time running around with buckets on their heads. That seems to be the favorite way for does around here to create excitement.

Every once in a while, someone knocks over a bucket of water. We have an automatic waterer and a large tub, but we also have individual buckets just in case. They hang from hooks. When empty, they make great rubbing posts. Soon someone rubs the empty bucket off its hook and onto the ground.

Someone else sticks her head inside and lifts up. The bail handle drops down over the back of the goat's neck, and she assumes she's stuck and goes running around the barnyard with a bucket on her head screaming and terrifying everyone else. You'd think the herd would be used to goats with buckets on their heads by now and ignore her. But no, her hysteria sends everyone else into hysteria. Eventually the bucket flies off and relative calm returns.

A yearling came up with a new twist on the old bucket trick. I heard horrendous, deafening screams coming from the barn and the sound of thirty multiplied by four hooves tearing around the wooden floor. The commotion was so extreme that I wondered if a cougar might be chasing my goats. Where were my guardian dogs?!

I rushed out to find a goat flopped on her side, thrashing futilely in an attempt to stand with a bucket not only over her head but with the bail hooked securely behind her elbows. She tried to stand but the bucket tripped her. Her screams were magnified inside the sounding box of a bucket as she lurched helplessly trying to get away from the terrifying monster that had grabbed her. I had to sit on the hysterical creature to disentangle her.

Getting stuck is just one way of causing trouble. Goats' voracious appetites get them into all sorts of trouble, from getting stuck trying to reach where they shouldn't, to escaping through fences, to trampling people who come between them and food.

During summer and fall, we feed comfrey daily to the goats. Comfrey is highly nutritious, green when nothing else is, and delectable to goats. So delectable that I can think of few things more dangerous than entering a herd of goats with an armload of comfrey. I make my husband do it.

I watch from the gate and marvel at Johnny's courage. He has developed a technique for getting in and back out alive. He quickly fights his way through the mob to the closest corner of the feeder, then slings the first bunch of comfrey to the far end. The goats all dash to that end, trampling and pushing each other out of the way. With quick flips, Johnny disperses the rest of the comfrey and then hightails it out of there before the goats can trample him.

It's quite an impressive operation to watch. If, however, Johnny's first fling falls short, he doesn't have time to rid himself of the rest of the comfrey before the herd is back on him. Then he has to resort to shouts and threats and curses and kicks, none of which have any effect at all.

My goats would go through fire to get to comfrey. They're certainly not going to let Johnny stand in their way.

The same thing happens with alfalfa pellets, on those rare occasions when I'm daring enough to feed them. I sneak into the barn with the can of pellets hidden under a jacket, then in one swift motion, pull the can out and fling pellets toward the far end of the feeder, spreading them as I throw. Immediately I jump back out of the way. Sometimes I'm successful. Other times I resort to shouting and threatening and cursing. I can't kick as there are too many goats standing on my feet.

You probably think I should have better behaved goats. You're right. My horses wouldn't think of crowding me. The goats think nothing of it. If I took the time to work with each doe individually, as I do the horses, perhaps they would politely wait for their feed. Perhaps.

But I wouldn't bet the rent. Goats and trouble just naturally go together.

THE GREAT ESCAPE

My mother always told me that pride goeth before a fall, so I guess it serves me right. I was inordinately proud of my roses and of my peach tree with its first crop ever of five yet-green peaches.

On that fateful morning, I headed for the barn in a cheerful mood. In spite of the heat, my garden and yard — especially the rose bed — were beautiful. I always stop to admire the roses on my way to the barn.

That awful morning I stopped and stared in horror. There were no rose flowers. No rose leaves, either. And the peach tree was lying on the ground.

It couldn't have happened. Not that. Not every goat owner's worst nightmare. But it had! The gate was open. The goats had been in the garden.

I screamed and ran to the house to get Johnny. I don't know what I thought he could do, but I screamed at him through the bathroom door then ran back outside to the peach tree. It was broken almost completely off, with its not-ready-to-be-picked peaches scattered about the ground. I was too upset to even cry.

Johnny came tearing out of the house, pulling his pants up and hollering, "What?! What?! Where are you?!"

"Over here!" I screamed.

He ran toward my voice, stopped, looked around and said, "What's wrong?"

"What's wrong?!" I bellowed. "What's wrong?! Don't you see anything wrong?!"

He looked at me and at the garden in bewilderment. I don't know what he expected from the tone of my voice but he obviously noticed nothing that should occasion such an uproar.

"Can't you see the peach?!" I screamed.

"Oh, yeah. Oh, no!" Even Johnny could see that a peach tree lying on the ground is not where a peach tree should be. "What happened?"

"The goats got out! They broke the peach tree and ate my roses," I cried.

Finally, Johnny saw that the roses looked somewhat different than they had the day before. The day before they had leaves and flowers. Today they had bare canes. Short bare canes.

We stood the poor peach upright and tied it to a stake, in hopes, by some miracle, it would survive. I picked up four premature peaches and one peach pit from the ground. So much for my first peach crop.

The reason the goats were only one gate away from the roses was because of my stupidity. I had opened the gate from their pasture so the goats could eat the brush in front of the barn. I had neglected to chain the gate going into the rose and peach area.

After the escape, the goats were locked three fences away from the rose garden.

I called a fellow goat breeder for sympathy. "I'm trying to decide if I should kill myself or the goats or both."

"Don't kill yourself," she counseled. "The roses will grow back better than ever. That's what my neighbor says every time my goats get out and eat her roses. But it's a shame about your peach."

I felt better after talking to her and hearing that her goats sometimes escaped, too. But the day wasn't over.

When I headed for the barn again, I saw one of the Muscovy ducks in the fenced vegetable garden, walking up and down the fence line, stomping on pea vines. The day before, the peas were climbing the fence. Now they were flat on the ground, under the pacing Muscovy.

"No!" I screamed. Johnny came charging back out of

the house, wondering what was wrong this time. We caught the duck and put him back in the adjacent chicken yard, then repaired every possible escape route, although there were none. Not even the bantam hens can get out of our chicken yard.

After the goats were milked, I plodded to the house, only to see the blasted Muscovy back in the garden, marching along the fence line again, smashing peas. That was when we learned that Muscovy ducks can fly. Since then, they've been locked in a covered cage during gardening season.

Even after goats and ducks were secured, my day was not over. As the thermometer soared into the 90's, I tried to untangle a hose from the backyard water spigot. Normally, I would carefully unwrap the hose. But I was in a foul mood, so I yanked. The hose came loose, but so did the water spigot. The pipe broke off below ground level and a geyser erupted in the back yard.

"Shoot," I said, or something quite similar, as I ran to shut off the well pump. Then I retired to the house and stayed there until Johnny came home. I'd done enough damage for one day.

The roses eventually grew new leaves. The peach died. For some time after the day of the Great Escape, it took a long time to get through all the gates I erected between garden and barn. (One friend said it was like entering a maximum security prison.)

Pride goeth before a fall and trust departs soon afterwards. After a herd of goats goes through, not much of anything remains.

GUARDIAN DOG
DRAWBACKS

Now don't get me wrong, I think livestock guardian dogs are wonderful. We have two and I wouldn't be without them. *But* . . . they are not without their drawbacks. At least, ours aren't.

When Anna came as a puppy to rescue our sheep, I was a bit apprehensive. And for good reason, as it turned out. Anna had not read the material I'd read that said she should stay in a pen with a ewe and lambs and should not be petted or else she'd bond to us rather than to the sheep.

Anna yowled and yipped and climbed the fence, dug under the fence, ate through the fence, and simply refused to stay put. We kept reinforcing until the entire pen was solid boards six feet high. She wiggled out when the door opened. But she did not run away or run to the house: she ran to the pasture where the main flock of sheep resided. So we gave up and let her stay there.

Alas, the excitement was not over. Anna thought lambs were marvelously fun companions. She dragged them around by their back legs and raced them around the field. (She was racing; they were fleeing in terror.)

I spent my days watching out the kitchen window and hollering whenever Anna started playing with the lambs. Other than mangling a few ears, she never hurt them; she just bounced. Our sheep were less than thrilled with a bouncing puppy. The goats wanted nothing what-soever to do with her. The does kept her far away from their kids.

But, we soon realized, the coyotes were no longer snacking on lambchops. Anna did what she was hired to do. But not the way we wanted. She did things her own way.

When a young coyote appeared in the field, Anna did not chase it away as we thought she should. She played with it. Coyote and Anna rolled and played tag and cavorted. But she never let it come anywhere near her flock. Before Anna came to live with us, we lost at least a dozen sheep and lambs each year to predators. We haven't lost a single one since.

But for several years, Anna did not understand the concept of private property. She assumed her territory was the entire valley, although I tried to show her the boundary lines and convince her to stay within them. Electric fencing worked but it was not possible to fence across the river and stream and through brushy wood-lands.

After Anna roamed onto a road a quarter mile away and was hit and seriously mangled (to the tune of a $500 repair job), she stayed home for a bit. And gradually, as she grew older, she simply stopped leaving. I don't know that we had much to do with her change of heart. I think she decided on her own that she had enough livestock to take care of on our forty-five acres.

When Anna was nine, she seemed considerably slowed down, so we decided to buy a pup for her to train. Anna disagreed with our decision from the day Finegan arrived. He was bouncy and wild and chewed her ears and tail and generally made a pest of himself. But Anna started losing her blubber and moving faster and, three years later, looked younger than she did when Finegan arrived.

She would have preferred to stay fat and slow. Anna tolerated Finegan, but that's about all.

Finegan never harassed the lambs or kid goats or

tried to chew his way out of things. Of course, as with a second child, we were more lenient. We didn't bother trying not to pet him and we didn't lock him in a pen with sheep or goats. We gave him to Anna.

She gave him back.

By this time, the guardian dog experts had changed their recommendations. Instead of telling us to keep our hands off these dogs, they said guardian dogs need attention and if they don't get enough at home will go elsewhere to find it. We didn't want to suffer through the wandering stage that Anna went through so we gave Finegan attention.

He is overwhelmingly friendly, either as a consequence of that attention or because it's just his personality. At least, he's friendly to us. However, he does his job.

Anna lives with the sheep. Finegan lives with the goats. The goats prefer Anna. She doesn't bounce as much. However, they run to hide behind Finegan whenever he sounds the alarm.

During the day, Finegan hangs out part of the time in front of the house, where he greets visitors (using the term "greet" loosely). Finegan is tail-wagging, lip-grinning friendly as soon as I say "It's okay". Before that, most first-time visitors stay in their cars.

Thankfully, Finegan finally passed the puppy stage where he chewed on everything in sight. Nevertheless, it is still unwise to lay down a pair of gloves. The chances are slim that five minutes later they will still be where you put them.

Although they don't hang out together, the two dogs work together when there is a threat anywhere. Both bark and run toward the threat, but one always stays close to their livestock family while the other tears off after the intruder. Usually Finegan leads the charge and barks and barks and barks and barks. Which leads us to the worst drawback of our guardian dogs — also one of the main reasons they are effective. Their lungs.

Anna has a deep, big dog bark that is not too annoying. She also barks only when necessary (although she barked more when she was younger). Finegan has a high-pitched bark, although he is even bigger than Anna. He has been known, many times, to bark all night. We have been known to get up umpteen times a night to shut him up before the neighbor complains. Finegan guards the entire property, which, to him, means treeing possums and coons and barking at them non-stop. Keeping him from annoying the neighbor is difficult.

We did, however, stop his raids on the neighbor's garbage can by electrifying the can. It only took once for Finegan to decide that a meal of garbage was not worth the effort. It also only took once to find out porcupines are not animals to put your mouth on. He was amazingly good for the torture of quill extraction.

Livestock guardian dogs are great at protecting livestock, lovingly tending new baby goats, and letting curious kids chew doggy tails but, like the rest of us, they have their faults. Their wanderlust and lungs can stretch a person's patience.

HUMBLE PIE

Why is it that the longer I have goats, the less I know? Every year my animals teach me how dumb I am.

I used to be able to tell when a doe was pregnant. It was easy: I just felt for the "cords" or ligaments on either side of the tail. They soften as the doe gets closer to kidding.

But one year Ember was so fat I couldn't tell if she was bred. "I'll be able to tell by her cords," I told myself. One day her cords seemed to be loosening. The next day, they weren't.

Well, if I lifted up on her abdomen in front of the udder, surely I could feel if there were kids inside or not. Wrong. She was too fat.

I asked everyone who came to the barn, "Do you think this doe is pregnant?"

"Heavens, yes," they all answered. "Looks like she'll have four."

That gave me hope. Although the year before everyone guessed Ember would have four and she had one.

As it turned out, Ember was not pregnant. She had taken a year off to get fatter even than usual. It took two years to slim her back down.

Pregnancy detection is not the only area where my confidence has been shattered. There's polledness. (Okay, so polledness isn't a word. Until now.) I use a naturally hornless (polled) buck on my (genetically, not actually) horned does and a horned buck on my polled does. So I never know what I'm going to get. However, polled heads are easy to spot, once you know how.

Or that's what I told the young woman who brought her doelings to me to have their horn buds taken off. She thought two of them might be polled, but she wasn't sure.

"I'll show you how to tell, even when kids are very young," I told her. "Come look at these triplet bucks that were just born. See? This one is polled and the other two will develop horns."

She couldn't see the difference.

"When you've seen enough of them," I assured her, "you'll be able to recognize a polled head immediately."

A month later, all three bucks (by then, wethers) still had no horn buds. They were all polled. Two of them never did develop the classic polled look, but they also never grew horns.

Even that embarrassment wasn't as bad as the ram fiasco. Someone I'd sold sheep to years ago called and asked if I'd like to buy her two-year-old colored ram. His mother was a ewe she'd bought from me; the sire unrelated. He was gentle, Mary assured me.

I'd been looking for a colored ram that was related to my flock so I said yes. The ram was lame when we brought him home, but Mary said he'd been fine a few days earlier. I penned him and examined his feet. He had a heel abscess in one, so I began a daily soaking routine. The ram was big, gentle and very wooly.

After two weeks of daily care, the abscess had nearly healed. The sheep shearer arrived. As the dark wool rolled off the ram's belly, the sheared stopped and said, "Well, lookee here! He's only got one ball! And his sack ain't long enough. Looks like they banded him and missed."

Sure enough, my beautiful, gentle ram had one testicle. I had never thought to check, or even to ask about his offspring. I called Mary. She assured me he sired lambs his first year, but, as it turned out, not the second.

Maybe as a yearling he had high enough fertility from that one testicle to breed ewes. But since he couldn't drop that testicle very far from his body to allow it to cool, probably the sperm was killed off most of the time. If I kept him naked all year, he might be able to settle ewes, but I wasn't willing to gamble.

I sold my lovely ram for meat. I spent a lot of time and effort healing the foot of an animal that I then sold at a loss for ramburger. Worse than the loss of money, though, was the loss of pride. What kind of livestock breeder buys a stud without checking his equipment? The sheep shearer is still guffawing.

UNANSWERABLES

Why is it that the longer I have goats, the fewer questions I can answer? For instance: "How long do you have to keep a momma-raised weanling away from her dam before she won't try to nurse again?"

I used to give a knowledgeable response to this question. I wish I could remember what it was. Now I say: "As long as it takes."

Sometimes it takes until you sell either the dam or her kid. That's why I sold Flourish. (Flourish is an odd name, I know. Her dam was Cherish. I couldn't think of anything else that ends in "ish." The following year Cherish had Embellish. Fortunately, Cherish died before kidding again. Beats me what I would have named her next doe kid.)

But as I was saying, I sold Flourish because she wouldn't stop nursing Cherish, even after Embellish was born. Before Embellish was born, I weaned Flourish. A few months after moving her into the pen of dry does, I put the dries back with the milkers because I needed that pen. Next milking, Cherish came into the milk room with no milk. She'd already been milked with a Flourish; a Flourish who had to be sold before her mother would dry up, just like Cherish's mother Cha Cha.

Cha Cha would milk, if you let her, for six years straight, spitting out kids every year without missing a milking. Cha Cha, however, cooperated by having mostly buck kids who left home at tender ages. Cherish was her last kid. If she'd arrived in Cha Cha's younger years, I might well have had three generations of goats nursing their dams: Embellish on Cherish on Cha Cha.

Which brings me to another unanswerable question: "How many goats do you need to supply a family of four with milk?"

Obviously, that all depends on how many generations of goats you have nursing on each other. You don't get much milk from a doe who is nursing her yearling daughter, believe me. Which is why I sold the yearling daughter. For once I had an answer to the question, "Why is this goat for sale?"

In years past, I explained that I kept two goats of each age for my show string and sold the rest. But since I quit showing, that answer doesn't fly. Theoretically, I now keep the best milkers who give me the least problems (or have the prettiest color, as I explain in another chapter). The truth is, I keep the goats I fall in love with. If a goat is for sale, it's because I'm not in love with her. Yet.

Unfortunately, I have a strange tendency to fall in love as soon as someone walks into my barn and wants to buy a goat. When I'm asked, "Why is this goat for sale?" I say, "I dunno. She's awfully nice, isn't she? Maybe I shouldn't sell her . . ."

This is why, I suspect, my long-suffering spouse follows me out to the barn these days when prospective buyers arrive. Before I can answer the fateful question: "Why is this goat for sale?" he chimes in with "Why aren't they all for sale? That's the real question."

The most common question that newbies ask, of course, is: "How do you tell when a doe is in heat?" They generally ask this in May. After I explain the breeding season of goats, the heat cycle, the signs, etc., I don't hear from them again until fall when they call and ask: "How do you tell when a doe is in heat?"

The only good answer is: "Ask a buck." All the other explanations —the tail wagging, the bleating, the mounting other goats, the buck rag in a bottle, etc. — are just useless words.

A lot of my advice over the years, I now realize, has been useless words. When asked, "How will I know when my doe is about to kid?" I would go on and on at great lengths about the signs of approaching parturition: the loosening ligaments on either side of the tail, the changing appearance of udder and teats, the floor pawing, the circling, blah, blah, blah.

Now I just say, "When you absolutely have to leave to go somewhere, that's when your doe will kid."

"Will she give birth without any trouble?"

"Yes, if it's the middle of a weekday when the vet is available to help. No, if she kids in the middle of the night, particularly a Saturday night."

"So what should I do?"

"Pray she kids during the week and not in the middle of a snowstorm when all the roads between you and the vet are closed."

Another much-asked question is: "What should I feed my goats?"

In years past, I explained the nutritional requirements of goats, the value of legume hay, the difference in grains, on and on ad nauseum. Now I say, "Feed them your roses."

And why not? That's what they're going to eat anyway. And if the people don't want the goats to eat their roses, I recommend a 4-H goat manual that will tell them what their goats need to eat to keep them happy enough to, hopefully, stay off the fence and away from the roses.

"What kind of fencing?" is another question I've stopped answering. Instead I respond with, "How badly do you want your roses?"

Maybe it's best that I no longer have the answers. Goats are much better teachers than I, and they will definitely and definitively answer all questions.

OPACCT

Every person, I've decided, has an optimal animal carrying capacity (OPACCT). Let me explain.

One year in particular, I made a concerted effort to cut the 30 or 40 goats in my barn down to a more reasonable number. After a summer of selling, Johnny was so impressed that he decided to count how many goats were left. He counted 35.

"Linda, there's something I don't understand. Before you started selling, you said you had 30 or 40 goats. I know you've sold at lest twenty, yet you still have 35. How come?"

"Gee, honey, I don't know. New math?"

The fact is, I never counted how many goats were in the barn. It looked like 30 or 40 to me. Apparently, I was wrong. That fall, after selling even more goats — a total for the year of fourteen milkers, three buck kids, thirteen doe kids and an undetermined number of wethers — I had 29 goats.

What I now believe is that 30 or 40 is my personal animal carrying capacity. I came to this conclusion because as soon as the goat numbers began to dwindle, a llama showed up in my back pasture. Then another Muscovy duck joined our single surviving one. A banty hen with six chicks appeared. Two geese turned into ten. It was almost like magic.

I am not the only one this has happened to. Indeed, it appears to be a universal phenomenon. A friend who went out of dairy goats some years ago soon went into angora goats. When those left, llamas arrived. She used to have four Saanen milkers and one buck. Now she has sixteen female llamas, seven stud llamas, and numerous crias (baby llamas). Not to mention her dogs, sheep, rabbits and geese.

Another friend sold her dairy goats because she wanted more time to ride her horse. Now she has six horses. She tells me she is going to sell at least two and never have that many horses again. I believe her. But I also believe she'll suddenly acquire canaries or guinea pigs or hedgehogs or something that eats and poops. (In fact, she did sell horses. But she then bought goats from me. Five years later, she again had six horses. Plus three goats.)

Through these experiences, I have stumbled upon what I believe to be a fundamental law of the universe, previously unrecognized. Maybe I'll win a Nobel prize. But never mind the glory, I just want to save all animal lovers everywhere a lot of trouble by explaining the implications of the Optimum Personal Animal Carrying Capacity Theory.

Especially, I want to explain the implications to the non goat-crazy mates of goat-crazy people: if they nag their partners into selling goats, their partners will be restless, unfulfilled and downright bitchy until their natural optimum animal carrying capacity is reestablished. In other words, if a person gets rid of goats, he'll get into something else. That something else might be even bigger and hungrier and more time-consuming than goats.

I know what some of you are thinking. You're thinking, "But Joe Blow used to have fifty goats and he hasn't even a dog now." I'm sure there are Joe Blows out there. Ask them how they feel. They might say, "Restless, unfulfilled and downright bitchy. But at least I'm not cleaning barns anymore."

They are living on memories, you can bet. Memories are good, but not good enough for most of us.

Non goat-crazy people have animal carrying capacities as well; their capacities just aren't as large as ours. I think I sold down that one year to below even Johnny's optimum capacity. No, he didn't encourage me to buy more goats, but one day he said, "You know, we don't have a water buffalo."

"This is true."

"A water buffalo would be nice."

"It would?"

"Sure. They're good eating. They can work. They're gentle. You can make cheese from their milk."

You see what might happen? Cut down your goat herd and the next thing you know, *presto,* you have a herd of water buffalo. All because you didn't understand one of the fundamental laws of the universe: OPACCT. Don't say I didn't warn you.

PART II

THOSE WONDERFUL, CRAZY GOATS and THEIR WONDERFUL, CRAZY PEOPLE

BARN FASHIONS

One of the finest aspects of goatkeeping is the clothes we get to wear. We get to wear whatever we want. There's no pawing through the closet for something clean and presentable in polite society. Goats are anything but polite. No shirts to iron, panty hose to pull on or shoes to buff. The goats don't care.

Footwear is the most critical element. For western Oregon, something that keeps one out of the mud is a necessity: rubber boots or clogs — or stilts, if you're coordinated enough. Personally, I lean toward sneakers in the summer and boots in the winter. Sometimes I wear tall rubber boots, sometimes short, lined, rubber boots. It all depends on the depth of mud and the degree of cold.

There are some fashion rules on the farm. No White is one of them. That rule is never disobeyed for long because whatever starts out white doesn't stay that way.

Although goat folk tend to wear jeans, I find coveralls over the jeans to be a necessity. Coveralls have so many wonderful pockets and compartments for stashing pocket knives and collars and goat goodies and syringes and hoof trimmers and bottles of iodine for dipping new navels. You name it, it has, at one time or another, been found in my coverall pocket.

My husband has often commented over the years on the unkempt state of my coveralls. I do tend to wear them to rags. This is because I hate to transfer all that pocket-stuff to a new pair. Johnny also comments when the smell becomes noticeable. When he thinks my coveralls are overdue for washing, he stands them up by themselves to prove his point.

I will empty pockets to occasionally wash coveralls, but I'm loathe to give up on a pair entirely. I did, once, though, after seeing myself in a photograph.

While visiting us, my brother took pictures of me with my beloved Morgan gelding. The horse looked great. I looked like someone who'd just been picked up from the side of the railroad tracks. Not only were my coveralls shredded, they were filthy and stained. Johnny says it's a good thing odors aren't transmitted on film. I'd like to show friends the photos of my horse but I can't cut me out of them because I'm on him.

The new coveralls that Johnny bought for me were brown. My old ones had all been some faded version of blue. This was good because, (whenever the weather dictated), I wore a faded blue denim jacket with my coveralls. I may have been ragged and dirty, but at least I matched.

With the new brown coveralls, a new jacket was a necessity. Especially since the old one was nearly as shredded as the old coveralls. So I began wearing what used to my mother's sort-of-suede leather chore jacket. It was quite a change from my normal attire. I liked it because it was big enough to cover my vest during cold weather but with the sleeves short enough not to catch streams of milk or dip into the wash water in the barn sink.

One cool spring day as I prepared to go outside, I caught a glimpse of myself in the mirror at the end of the hall. I looked amazingly spiffy in my new brown coveralls, new old tan jacket, and knit hat with trim that exactly matched the jacket. The effect would have been somewhat more stunning if the coveralls fit.

I understand the baggy look is in these days, but these coveralls were rather extreme. The crotch hung just above my knees and the legs were rolled six times in an unsuccessful attempt to keep them out of the mud. Johnny has a rather grandiose idea of my size, I think, as he always buys me gargantuan coveralls.

The brown coveralls met their demise rather suddenly the June day I fell off my Mr. Smith and broke shoulder blade, collar bone, and ribs. The EMTs who arrived at the house to pick up what remained of me, cut my coveralls off. I haven't worn the brown jacket since. It doesn't match the new blue coveralls.

One winter I joined the goat-barn fashion elite when I finally broke down and put on the incredibly warm and lovely insulated coveralls Johnny bought me several years before. (I'm not getting fashion conscious in my old age, I'm just getting colder.)

I can wear the insulated coveralls only in the very frostiest weather. After fifteen minutes of any sort of activity at all, I'm sweating inside them. Even in the light-weight blue coveralls, there is often a trail of discarded clothing scattered here and there as I heat up doing chores.

The hat is the first to go, usually as soon as I start cleaning the barn. After one trip through the mud with a full wheelbarrow, the jacket comes off. If the barn cleaning takes very many trips, the vest is shed.

As any goat person knows, the trick is to stow these articles of clothing where the goats and dogs can't get to them. Our livestock guardian dogs have a passion for hats and gloves.

Goats, of course, have a passion for anything made of cloth or yarn. The kids are the worst. They don't even wait for me to carelessly lay down my hat. If I lean over to their level, they pull it right off my head.

Then begins the game of "Catch me if you can!" The more I try, the more they flee. If a kid happens to fling the hat as she runs, someone else picks it up. It becomes a relay race with my hat the loser.

Not just dogs and goats eat hats. I'll never forget the time the lawn mower ate my favorite barn hat. I was devastated. Some of us grow quite attached to our barn clothes. After all, some of us live in close proximity with our clothes for many years. Through happy and sad times, our clothing stands by us (sometimes literally).

I hate parting with old, shredded coveralls, and it isn't just because I have to clean out the pockets. Over the years, they become part of me. (Johnny says they wouldn't have if I'd take them off and wash them more often.)

One of these days, I'll break out the brand new coveralls I bought for goat shows some years ago. It must have been some years ago because I haven't shown since 1996. You never know, though, when I might decide to start showing again. It would be a shame to have used up those pretty coveralls.

A WEEK WITH BERNIE

People who agree to farm-sit for us need a good sense of humor. Quite a few of our farm sitters start out with a sense of humor, but lose it after three days with my goats. Nubians tend to do that to people. Bernie kept his for an entire week. That's a record.

Spirit and Choice were well-behaved for me and Johnny. They were terrified of everyone else. So they ran away. It's hard to keep smiling when the goats you are supposed to be milking won't come into the barn to be milked. Or so say our farm sitters when they explain why they won't ever farm-sit for us again.

In the fall of 1994 we visited our son in college in Pennsylvania. We were gone for six days. None of our former farm sitters were available that week, for some suspicious reason. So we employed a new one.

Bernie used to raise Nubians, but hadn't owned goats for quite some years. He came a week before we were to leave and went through the entire milking and feeding procedure. Bernie petted and admired the goats. Most rubbed against him companionably. Spirit and Choice ran away.

Bernie assured me he'd have no problem. When I called the day after we'd left, Bernie said he was having a great time. But he hadn't slept well the first night because Anna (our only livestock guardian dog at the time) barked that night. In the morning, all the goats and sheep were still alive, so he figured she must have taken care of whatever was causing her to bark. I agreed and told him not to worry: Anna often barked at night.

The water heater didn't help Bernie's sleep pattern either. He wasn't sure if it was about to explode or if it always sounded like a space shuttle on take-off. The water heater is rather noisy, now that I think about it. Guess I'd grown used to it. Plus, Johnny and I sleep at the north end of the house. The water heater and Bernie were at the south end.

"Oh well, ha ha," said Bernie. "As long as your water heater is supposed to sound like a boiler about to blow, I won't worry. I'll just jam a pillow over my ears."

"Gee, I'm sorry, Bernie. Are there any other problems?"

"Problems? No problems."

"What about Spirit and Choice?"

"I caught them eventually. Then I locked them in an empty pen overnight and led them to the milk stand this morning. I gave them lots of extra attention after milking before letting them out with the others. Maybe they'll be easier to catch tonight."

They weren't. Every night Bernie milked the other goats first, then threw down hay and caught Spirit and Choice when their greed overcame their terror and they buried their heads in the hay manger. At night he kept them locked in a pen. In the day he let them graze with the herd. It wasn't an ideal situation, but it was better than having to chase two goats twice a day.

The last time we talked on the phone before returning, Bernie was still having a good time. Or so he said.

When we arrived home in Oregon, the farm was in great shape. Bernie had picked tomatoes from the garden for us, cleaned the barn daily without being asked, and left a letter thanking us profusely for allowing him to stay on the farm. Bernie seemed too good to be true. Then I read the rest of the letter.

"I thought it would be fun to do fruit basket upset, so I let all of the goats out of their various pens and put them all together just to see if I could sort them out again. They had a great time together, butting heads, climbing on top of each other, and all the other good stuff goats do when they get together for a family reunion. I hope they didn't have too much fun. You'll have to tell me how I did on the sorting process.

"Also, I knew you would want any of your does who came in heat to be bred. Since I didn't know where the A-I stuff was, I decided to use the buck. Actually, I should say bucks, because since I didn't know which buck you wanted to use, I let all the bucks in with the herd. You can probably figure out which buck sired the kids next year by doing a DNA test. Hope this was okay.

"Which does came in heat? I'm not even sure, but you will be able to tell five months from this weekend. Oh, I have had fun. I'm sure you will want me to come back the next time you are away."

For an instant, my heart dropped into my stomach. But then I realized that Bernie was joking. Perhaps teasing me with his wild tale of goat-basket upset was Bernie's way of paying me back for the uncooperative goats and roaring water-heater.

Oddly enough, after that week on our farm, Bernie was always busy when I asked him to farm-sit.

EVERYBODY
NEEDS A MOM

This is the strange story of an Alpine breeder turned Nubian owner and a draft horse raised on goats.

A friend of mine, Dorothy, bought a beautiful, huge, Suffolk draft mare in foal. Six days after the very large, lovely filly was born, the mother died quite suddenly from a twisted intestine.

Dorothy began feeding the orphaned filly the milk replacer her veterinarian recommended. The filly scoured. (Scours are otherwise known as diarrhea.) Years before, Dorothy had raised Alpines and had learned the value of goat milk in raising orphan animals. Baby animals tend to find goat milk easier to digest than commercial formulas.

It so happened that earlier in the spring Dorothy had bought a milking Nubian, Muriel, from me. She wanted her two teenaged daughters, who had been mere babies when Dorothy sold her Alpines, to learn the joy of milking. Dorothy began feeding Muriel's milk to Comet, the filly. The scours cleared up.

However, a Suffolk filly is supposed to get three gallons of milk a day. Muriel was not producing three gallons. Not even close. So Dorothy came over and bought two more goats: Spumoni and Dreamweaver. Unfortunately, all I had left to sell were yearlings.

Dorothy thought it would be easier if Comet would nurse from the goats instead of a bottle, so she raised the milk stand high, built a ramp, and gave it a try. The goats never flinched when this enormous animal, with a head far bigger than any udder, nursed. The filly was delighted.

However, Comet still wasn't getting enough milk. So Dorothy found a goat person close to her with surplus milk and began supplementing. Or trying to. The filly refused to take the bottle. Finally, Dorothy tricked her into nursing by holding the bottle between the teats of whatever goat was on the milk stand. I have a video of a huge baby horse drinking from a bottle between Muriel's legs while Muriel eats grain. When the bottle was empty, Dorothy let Comet nurse. Muriel just stood there.

But horses drink very slowly from bottles. At least, Comet did. Dorothy got tired of holding the bottle, especially in such an awkward position, especially six times a day, which is how often the filly had to be fed. So she bought a fourth goat from me. Cinnamon was also a yearling, but she provided just enough more milk so the bottle could be discarded.

Comet and goats lived together in the same large pen. Comet would try to sneak drinks from the goats when they were not on the milk stand but they evaded her. About a week after the goat nursing operation began, Dorothy called, quite excited. "Spumoni is letting Comet nurse in the stall!"

A week later, she called again to tell me a friend had been over and asked if the goats allowed that big baby to nurse.

"Only one allows it: Spumoni."

"So that must be Spumoni," said the friend, pointing to a goat that was calmly standing while Comet suckled. It was not Spumoni. It was Cinnamon.

Cinnamon, as the last goat to arrive and the smallest, was on the bottom of the pecking order. Whenever the other goats picked on her, she ran to hide under Comet's belly.

"She doesn't even have to duck," said Dorothy.

Cinnamon and Comet became inseparable. Comet was by now nearly three times as tall as her yearling goat mother. The filly still nursed from Spumoni as well, but Spumoni didn't mother Comet — or hide under her.

As time went by, Dorothy wanted Comet to eat more horse feed and less milk. So she sold Spumoni and Dreamweaver, keeping Cinnamon and Muriel. Everywhere Comet went, so went Cinnamon. Everywhere Cinnamon went, Muriel followed.

Early that fall, the six of them (Comet, Cinnamon, Muriel, Dorothy and her two daughters) went on a camping trip. They all had a wonderful time. Comet was still nursing from Cinnamon, although the little yearling didn't have much milk anymore.

That worried Dorothy. As long as the filly and Cinnamon were in the same pasture, Comet followed her around until Cinnamon stopped and moved her rear leg back so Comet could fit that enormous head below the goat's belly and suck her dry. Dorothy decided enough was enough and separated the goats and horse.

Nobody was happy with this solution. This was bad because when Cinnamon was unhappy, she was loud. She was a Nubian, after all.

Alpine breeders will likely think that even more amazing than having a draft horse nurse from a goat is having an Alpine owner converted to Nubians. Let me reassure you: Dorothy had not been converted. Not originally. Her daughters wanted the Nubian.

Then when the filly was orphaned, Dorothy didn't want to bring aggressive Alpines on the place for fear they'd murder Muriel. Wisely, she bought from the same herd Muriel came from so there were not many adjustments to be made. Except by Dorothy.

"When Comet gets out of her sight, Cinnamon sounds like she's being tortured." Dorothy told me.

"Yep," I said. What else could I say? Cinnamon was a Nubian.

Dorothy assured me she wasn't really complaining.

After all, the goats had saved Comet's life. Even the veterinarian agreed.

In a few years, Dorothy's older daughter grew up and went away to college, taking Comet with her. Dorothy sold Cinnamon.

But Muriel stayed. Dorothy was in love. Dorothy swears Muriel is the perfect goat, even if she is a Nubian. An Alpine breeder turned soft on a Nubian proves that miracles happen.

A GOOD HOME
FOR A GOAT

One discouraging thing about raising and selling goats is the homes they're sold to. It's not that they're bad homes; it's just that they're often not lasting ones. People go in and out of goats as fast as children grow in and out of clothes. The good home becomes a good but goatless home and the goats they bought from me become someone else's.

For a few years, I asked for the first right to buy a goat back after it left my farm. But I never really wanted a goat back. I always have too many as it is.

Even people who stick with the goat project may not stick with the goats they bought from me. Many people keep the kids they raise and sell the dams they purchased. I don't blame them. It's just that I hate the thought of my goats being shuffled around.

Sometimes, though, the second new home is an improvement. And sometimes, when the goat and I are very lucky, both homes are wonderful. Such was the case for Cinnamon.

Cinnamon was one of the goats that friend Dorothy bought to supply her orphaned draft horse filly with milk. Since Dorothy wanted the goats to produce as much as possible for the giant baby, she fed them the choicest alfalfa plus several other types of hay to make sure they had everything they wanted. Cinnamon and her compatriots were in goat heaven.

But once the filly was weaned, the goats needed new homes. Cinnamon found Hazel.

Hazel and her family had never had a goat before. She called me the first day and said, "We're so worried about Cinnamon. She seems so depressed. We're afraid she'll get sick. Maybe, since she came from your farm, we should come buy a goat from you to keep her company."

Cinnamon was due to produce her own company in a week, so I explained that a new goat would also be lonely for its old home, and they might just compound their problem. And so Hazel decided that one or another member of her family would live with Cinnamon until she kidded.

Cinnamon thrived on the attention. She soon delivered three bouncing, healthy babies. With plenty to keep her occupied, Cinnamon no longer needed undivided attention from humans. This was good because her humans had fallen in love with the babies and were now heaping attention on them, instead of Cinnamon.

Then disaster struck. Cinnamon came down with peritonitis. The veterinarian didn't hold out much hope — but then, he hadn't counted on the nursing care Cinnamon was to receive.

A week later, with 24-hour attention, Cinnamon was back to normal, eating all the tasty tidbits her devoted owners had tried to tempt her with while she was ailing. Only the fresh-produce stand's finest cauliflower, broccoli, asparagus, lettuce, etc., came home for Cinnamon. The family spent more on food for that goat than for themselves.

But Cinnamon's milk production didn't go back up sufficiently after sickness to feed all three babies. So Hazel and family came to my farm and bought a milker. "She'll cry for a week," I warned them. But Lady Jane never had the opportunity.

"She cries when we leave the barn, so someone stays with her," Hazel explained.

Fortunately, it took a bit less than a week for Lady Jane and Cinnamon to bond, or at least get used to each other enough so that Lady Jane quit screaming for people. Lady Jane eventually adopted one of Cinnamon's babies. Hazel was thrilled.

"I could sit all day watching the goats," she told me. "I want more." I tried to warn her that goatkeeping is fully as addictive as chocolate and much more expensive. But there was no use. Hazel soon had more goats.

Lady Jane remained her most vocal goat, but Hazel loved her anyway. And Hazel still calls me to say, "Cinnamon did the cutest thing today . . ." or, "The goats just came running down the hill, leaping and twisting. They are so beautiful! I could watch them all day."

Lucky goats. Lucky me.

FUNNY PHONE CALLS

Being known as the "goat person" of the area has its benefits. For one thing, there are the funny phone calls. People ask the strangest things.

"Hello, I'm new to goats and someone gave me your number. I hate to bother you but could you answer a question?"

"Sure, I'll try!"

"My goat rolls her head and neck around all the time. Is this what I've read is the circling disease?"

For this one, I had to ask some questions of my own to figure out what she was talking about. No, the doe wasn't walking in circles or pushing her head against objects (as she might with listeriosis, commonly called "the circling disease"). She was standing in one place, twisting her neck in the air.

"Sounds like a Nubian," I quipped.

"Why, she *is* a Nubian! Is this a common disease with them?"

"Well, that behavior is common to some Nubians. But it might be common to others, too. I only raise Nubians. Come to think of it, though, we had an Alpine cross years ago that did that."

"Did she survive?"

"Well, I suppose she's dead by now. We sold her because she jumped fences."

"But my goat does this head circling thing all the time. It really has me worried."

"Maybe she has ear mites. Or maybe she's just bored."

I told her about my brother-in-law's experiment. Bruce, a non-farm guy, was fascinated one visit by the head-twisting ability of my goats, so he held a comfrey leaf over the head of one of the more athletic (and greedy) members of my herd. As the doe reached for the leaf, Bruce moved it in a circle. She followed the leaf, twisting her neck nearly 360 degrees.

Bruce is a sculptor by trade. Our front porch now sports a wood statue of a goat reaching for the door bell, her neck twisted nearly all the way around.

Another caller this fall was quite excited. "Our doe is in heat! The ram sheep stuck his nose to her butt and she squatted and peed! Can we bring her over quick? I'm afraid the ram will breed her!"

Not grasping the significance of the peeing, I asked how she knew her goat was in heat.

"She peed when the ram sniffed her!"

"Well, did the ram then act excited?"

"No, not really."

"If she were in heat, a buck, and probably a ram, would know by the smell of her urine. Is she flagging her tail or making more noise than usual?" (This was a dangerous question since the person calling was friend Hazel and the goat in question was Lady Jane, the mouthy Nubian she bought from me.)

"No, I don't think so."

"I don't think Lady Jane is in heat, Hazel. Wait until she starts flagging and crying and other goats start mounting her or she tries to mount them."

"But she peed when the ram sniffed her."

"She probably would do that any time the ram stuck his nose where she didn't think it belonged."

A week or so later, Hazel called again and said Lady Jane started screaming in the middle of the night and every time anyone touched her rump her tail went back and forth like crazy and the doe's best friend was climbing on her. This doe was anything but subtle about her condition. They brought her over that morning and my buck happily serviced her.

Another caller was worried because her doe's tail was held flat down against her body. "All the other goats tails are up. I think she's sick."

"Is she off feed? Standing by herself? Hunched up? Shivering?"

The answer was no, the doe was acting normally except for her tail. But the caller never did accept that the doe either 1) had some goop sticking her tail to her body or 2) had some irritant that made her clamp her tail down or 3) just felt like holding it that way. The caller decided it was because the doe was pregnant and had morning sickness. Fine, give her a saltine.

And then there was the lady who wanted to know, after I told her she needed to have her goats tattooed before registering them, if she could pick the tattoo.

"Well, usually people register their herd letters with the American Dairy Goat Association for use in the right ear, and put an identifying year and number tattoo in the left ear."

"Oh, I thought you meant a tattoo, you know, like a heart with an arrow through it."

Now that is an idea I'd never considered.

Many callers come up with things I haven't considered. For instance, "Will raccoons eat baby goats?"

The caller had seen a raccoon near her barn one day. She feared it would eat the two new baby goats she had just bought and was bottle feeding. She couldn't put them with the big goats because the big goats butted them, so the babies were in a stall by themselves. But it wasn't a raccoon-proof stall, she was sure.

Although I've never heard of a raccoon eating a baby goat, I really couldn't say definitively that it could never happen. After all, coons eat chickens.

"Don't you have a dog on your place?"

"Yes, two, but we bring them in the house at night to scare away intruders."

I didn't get anywhere with the suggestion that the

dogs would scare intruders away before they ever entered the house if she left the dogs outdoors. Last I heard, the dogs were still in the house at night and the baby goats were still alive and well. So, some questions go unanswered:

"*Will* raccoons eat baby goats?" and

"Why *not* a heart with an arrow through it?"

GOAT ROPING

Instead of hauling goats from one county fair to the next one summer, I stayed home. The purpose was to give myself and the goats a rest and to catch up on the non-goat portion of my life. A side benefit was that I was home when company came. It was fun seeing friends instead of just hearing Johnny tell me about them.

As it turned out, I never again rode the show circuit, other than a last try at the National Show the following year. But that's another story.

One couple who visited that first fair-free summer, 1994, were friends from twenty-seven years back, when we lived in Wyoming. Garth hadn't changed much. He was still full of stories, mostly about his infamous horse trades. This time, though, he also told a goat story.

When Garth was a kid growing up in Utah, he liked to practice roping. So did his best friend, Scott. Garth's dad didn't appreciate the kids roping his calves, so he bought a $5 goat.

"You can't hurt a goat like you can calves," said Garth.

At this point in the story, I protested, as Garth knew I would.

"Watch out, Garth," cautioned his wife, Maydene. She had witnessed my tangles with her husband years before over whether my horse, Imp, was spoiled or Garth was a lousy rider. Imp never bucked *me* off.

"As I was saying," Garth went on, "you can't hurt a

goat, but they're smart. They're smarter than sheep or dogs or horses . . ."

"Or would-be cowboys," I interjected.

"That goat soon learned if he didn't run, I couldn't chase and rope him. But he'd follow my friend Scott anywhere. So I talked Scott into running ahead with the goat a-high-tailin' after him. Then I'd gallop up and rope the goat. Sometimes I would catch the goat, sometimes Scott, and sometimes I would run over both of them. But that was okay. Scott was tough and you can't hurt a goat."

When Garth turned sixteen, he decided he just had to have a car. "My friend Steve had this 1929 Studebaker called C l a r a b e l l e . Clarabelle didn't run but I was sure I could get her running. Steve needed $25 for a rodeo entry fee and offered to sell me Clarabelle for that amount. I told him I'd give him all the money I had. He said, 'Okay, how much you got?' I had $23. 'Nah, that ain't enough," he said.

"Well, I got that roping goat, too,' I told him.

"'Okay, give me the goat and your $23 and you can have Clarabelle.'

"So there went my roping goat. Steve never could use that goat for roping, though, 'cause without Scott, the goat wouldn't run. And Scott wouldn't run for anybody but me."

Garth still has Clarabelle. She never did run either. Although Garth now insists that she did and, furthermore, that he's still driving her. "I drive Clarabelle to church all the time. If you don't go to church too often, a car will last a long time."

At the time of his visit to our farm in 1994, Garth was horseless. I'm sure it didn't last long. I'll bet as soon as he returned from vacation, he headed for the auction yard. Garth never could stay away from auctions. That's where he'd bought the last horse he owned.

"Boy, she was a pretty little mare. Arab. Looked a little rough at the sale barn, like somebody put her out on dry pasture and forgot about her, but I could see she'd be a nice horse with a little feed. I couldn't stand to see her go for meat so I bid on her. Got that mare for $400. Took her home, saddled up, stepped on, and she threw me right back off."

Maydene laughed and said, "That mare could go every which way I didn't know a horse could go."

"Finally got her calmed down enough to ride," said Garth, "but you could never relax. Had to be on your toes every minute. Kind of like that spoiled horse of yours, Linda, what was his name?"

"Imp, and he wasn't spoiled."

"Yes, that's right, Imp. That horse sure was spoiled. Anyhow, that Arab mare 'bout killed Maydene, here, when she tried to ride her.

"I got to looking at her one day and all of a sudden I recognized her — the mare I mean, not Maydene. She was a horse I'd sold seven years before! She was unrideable then, too, and hadn't improved with age. That little spitfire had likely been out on pasture ever since the guy I sold her to tried riding her."

Garth didn't say, but I'll bet he sold that mare for a whole lot more than he paid for her — either time — and probably with quite a story to go with her. I think that's what people paid for when they bought horses from Garth

— the stories. The horses sure weren't worth much.

Come to think of it, I've known quite a few goat people like Garth. They milked their stories for a whole lot more than they ever got out of their goats.

Garth justifies his horse-trading by saying: "I like horse sales. They're a lot like a Sunday School class. The more you participate, the more you learn. But you got to be careful at a horse sale 'cause lots of the animals are spoiled like that Imp horse."

Garth seldom kept a horse more than a year or two. He didn't like the horses so much as the trading of them. He says, "You should keep the same wife but always look for a better horse. Lots of people have that backward anymore.

"A man really don't need much in life to be happy. He just needs a good woman, a good horse, and a few good friends.

"I just need a little better horse."

Not being a horse trader like Garth, I left my beloved Imp out on range at Garth's ranch back in 1967, when Johnny and I went overseas for a year. That was two years before we got into goats. My folks picked Imp up later on and trailered him to Oregon.

"We had a devil of a time loadin' that horse," Garth told me again that 1994 visit. He's told me that about thirty times now and I've only seen him five times since we returned from overseas.

"That fool horse got his front feet clear up in the manger of your dad's trailer and we couldn't get him down. You must have spoiled that horse bad."

"I never had trouble loading Imp. Dad said he was squirrelly the whole trip. You must have ruined him. I trailered him lots after that without any problems."

"Well, sure," Garth said. "You had him so spoiled that he thought he was a person."

I'm going to find a suitable horse for Garth before his next visit and take him riding. Anybody who ropes goats and says you can't hurt them needs a come-uppance. Too bad Imp is in horse heaven. Wonder if that little Arab mare is still around?

LESSONS IN HUMILITY

Cha Cha, at age six, taught me just how smart goats are, and how dumb I am. She freshened in December with a single doe kid whom she adored.

When the baby was about six months old, Cha Cha quit bounding into the milk room, as was her habit. Instead she made me chase her down, then drag her in. Up on the milk stand, she cried and refused to eat. Her udder, normally part empty because of her nursing kid, was full. I worried that something had happened to her baby, but, no, Cherish was fine.

This went on for a week. Cherish was obviously not nursing, yet she was not sick. Cha Cha had weaned her kid, yet she was more solicitous of her than ever.

Then one morning when I opened the milk room door, there was Cha Cha with Cherish at her side. Both came leaping in. Cherish jumped on the milk stand (I have a two-holer) next to her mom. Since she was on the stand, I figured I might as well feed her grain, so I did. Immediately, Cha Cha, who had not eaten for a week, devoured her food.

Could this be what she wanted? Having weaned her kid, did Cha Cha expect me to start feeding her daughter grain on the milk stand? From that day forward, the two came into the milk room together and both ate just fine.

I think Cha Cha was a very smart goat: it took her only a week to train me.

Then came the National Show in Salem, Oregon, just 35 miles down the road. This was in 1995. I took Cherish, but not Cha Cha, who had never pretended to be show quality. Cherish adapted well to her pen at the fairgrounds with all the other kids. Back home, Johnny told me Cha Cha was in a deep depression and would not eat.

I came home twice during that week and coaxed some food into Cha Cha, telling her over and over that her baby would be back soon. She just lay in a corner of the barn and stared into space. I felt terrible.

Finally we were home and the two were reunited. I watched as all the goats that had been at the show mingled and butted heads with their stay-at-home friends. Cha Cha, after nuzzling her baby, came up to me and rubbed her head on my side, then gazed lovingly into my eyes. I'd kidnapped her beloved daughter, but instead of holding a grudge, Cha Cha thanked me for returning her. As usual around my goats, I felt humbled.

The National Show was also a humbling experience. Never in my life have I seen so many gorgeous goats in one place. I have no idea how the judges sorted them into placings: I thought they were all beautiful.

And to think I spent hours at home trying to decide which goats to bring. The one with the too-short ears or the one with the straight face? The one with the too-steep rump or the one that was close at the hocks? I should have left them all home and just watched the show.

But there's something about being a part of a National Show that you just can't get as a spectator. Tired, dirty, and discouraged come to mind. Ah, but the memories.

I'll never forget the Aurora incident. Finding her mom, Deb, in the bleachers, Aurora said, "Me and Starr have to go home."

"Why?" asked Deb.

"Because the hair fell off her face."

"What?"

"The hair fell off Starr's face and the blade wash fell in the milk bucket."

"Sounds like someone was clipping her face."

"No," Aurora insisted. "The hair just fell off."

"Okay, we'll talk about it later, Aurora. I want to watch the show."

"I'm awful tired, Mom. I'm going to the camp to take a nap." With that, Aurora disappeared.

When Deb went to her pens later, she found a sight that reduced her to helpless laughter. Deb called me over to her pens, laughing uncontrollably, and pointed out Aurora's doe. Starr's head had two closely shaved areas, as though someone had taken a very short blade and made two swipes. It looked like one of those modern haircuts.

It would have seemed funnier to me if I hadn't done the very same thing in my early years of showing goats. Not knowing the different blade sizes, I'd clipped with a #10, then decided to use something closer on the face. What I had was a #40. The goat was pure black. At least she was before I shaved a strip on her nose. Suddenly she was black with a bald, gray stripe.

Unlike Aurora, I didn't have enough sense to stop with one or two swipes. Instead, I shaved her whole head. Total

Eclipse had a very hooked Nubian nose when I started. When I finished it was even more so. Plus her head was now dull, bald gray while the rest of her was shiny black.

The judge laughed himself silly. I explained that I started with a too short blade and thought I'd better finish with that. He said, between guffaws, that I should have quit with the single swipe — but my goat sure had good breed character! Ha ha ha!

I don't know when I've been so humiliated.

So I felt for Aurora and her attempts to beautify her goat. As it turned out, Aurora didn't get to show Starr, her only goat at the National Show, anyway. When the tattoos were checked after the milk-out, the last of the three letters in her ear was hard to read. The bottom of the L was not discernible, said the powers that be. Deb asked if they could retattoo her.

Absolutely not, she was told. No retattooing at the National Show. I couldn't see how it would hurt to let an 8-year-old child show her goat, especially since it was obvious what the tattoo was supposed to be, but rules are rules and Deb is the kind of person who walks a straight path through life and teaches her children to do the same.

Aurora was heartbroken. After all, she'd been planning on this for a long time. It's a pretty exciting thing for an 8-year-old to show her goat at the National Show, a show that hadn't been to Oregon in 13 years — since long before Aurora was born! Starr probably would not have made the top twenty, but neither did a lot of other wonderful goats (including most of mine).

However, Aurora recovered and gamely showed one of her sister's goats instead. It's not the same as showing the doe you've had since she was born — your showmanship goat — the doe you clipped yourself. But Aurora accepted the situation.

Again, I was humbled. Goats humble me with great regularity. Occasionally, a goat owner does, too. Goats know what is really important in life. So do some goat people — like Deb and her daughter Aurora.

LINDA FINK GOATS

In winter, my goats spend a lot of time hanging out in the barn getting on each other's nerves. Awesome, in particular, dislikes close company. She always seems to be ticked at someone. One of her most frequent adversaries is a doe named Vision. The two will go at it head and hoof for what seems like hours.

Sonata, Awesome's adult daughter, usually joins her mom to gang up on Vision. Sometimes Vision's sister Dreamdance will help out, but just as often as Dreamdance defends her sister, she turns on her.

The weanlings (who aren't weaned) mimic their moms and aunts, having sparring sessions of their own. Whenever one moves too close to the primary combatants, a milker indicates the doeling's place in the order of things by bashing her.

The youngsters are not nearly so serious about their arguments as the adults. They tend to forget to butt, instead leaping upward and sideways while twisting their bodies in exuberance. Then the whole lot of them takes off at breakneck speed, Nubian ears flying, dashing about the paddock with occasional caprioles and courbettes. (I wonder why no one has tried to do dressage with goats. Their airs above ground are spectacular.)

The oldest goats are usually the peacemakers, moving between battling pairs whenever the fight grows heated. Diedra used to be one of the most aggressive fighters, but with age has come tolerance. Now, as Vision and Awesome fight, Diedra steps between them, separating them, distracting them, cocking her head at whomever is being the nastiest. It doesn't stop the fight but it calms it down. As soon as Diedra is satisfied that no one is going to permanently damage anyone else, she returns to the hay bunk.

Some goats never join the battlefield. Ember is one who has always disdained physical exertion of any kind. The only muscles she cares to exercise are in her jaw. Obese Ember hasn't wind enough to talk, much less fight.

Others, however (being Nubians), do talk, especially when in heat. But noisy Nubians are not tolerated inside the barn even by Nubians, at least not in my barn. So when someone comes in heat and bellows all day, the others relegate her to the outdoors.

One little doeling came into heat without saying a word. Instead, she fixed her desire on Diedra, who wanted no part of her. Why this kid decided Diedra was a buck I'll never know. She followed the older doe everywhere, flagging her tail like crazy, begging to be mounted. Diedra clobbered the baby over and over but still the kid came back for more.

If the doeling had been bleating, the other milkers would have helped Diedra banish her from the barn. But she was quiet. And persistent.

Herds with fewer does do not always have disciplinarians to keep the loudmouths in check. I recently sold a doe kid to some folks with one other kid in their barn. I told Bruce and his wife that their new kid would probably cry for a week. That's how long it generally takes for my goats to adjust elsewhere.

Two days later, my friend Hazel called and said, "I just met the people you sold a goat to this weekend."

Hazel happens to live across the street from the new buyers. She told me that she'd heard a woman calling for help from that direction. Over and over the woman, in a very distressed voice, yelled "HELP! HELP!"

Hazel was afraid to go across the street and see what was wrong. Maybe, she thought, the husband was beating his wife and would attack Hazel, too. But the awful sound went on and on, so Hazel finally called 911. Then she anxiously awaited the arrival of police. And waited and waited.

When she could wait no longer, Hazel summoned all her courage, climbed in her car and drove slowly past the house. A man was working in front of the house and, since she no longer heard the screams, she cautiously rolled down her window and said, "Excuse me, but I thought I heard a woman calling for help over here. Did you hear it?"

"Oh, that must have been our goat," said Bruce. "We just bought her from Linda Fink."

An embarrassed Hazel explained that the police might be driving up any second. Bruce was very nice about it. He said "Better safe than sorry." They talked until an officer finally arrived. He checked out the story and left, laughing.

Hazel apologized, then suggested that her neighbor post a sign on his front lawn: "The sound you hear is a Linda Fink goat."

Last I heard, Lady Jane, the noisy goat Hazel bought from me, and the homesick kid across the road were communing with each other at great volume. I would think that Hazel's other goats would grow sick of the noise and mutiny.

But they haven't. And Hazel is threatening to put up signs on both sides of the road saying "The sounds you hear are Linda Fink goats."

THE STORY OF MIKEY

"Life," Liz Rishel told me, "is a series of challenges that help you grow." Liz is the long-time dairy goat superintendent of the Oregon State Fair and has been in goats forever. She gave me this piece of wisdom as I was in her motel room during the 1996 fair, recovering from an attack of Meniere's Syndrome. Meniere's Syndrome, an odd condition of the inner ear that makes you so dizzy you vomit for hours, was the challenge that began the year after my back accident and three years before my horse accident.

I don't know how much growing I've done from all these challenges, but I've certainly learned how wonderful goat folk are when someone needs help. When the world started spinning at the Oregon State Fair and I had to retreat from my job as ring steward, everyone jumped to the rescue. Bev and her daughter took over in the ring, Sher tended me, brought me a cot, held my hand, and did many things above and beyond the call of friendship. Shari provided the medication that helped pull me out of it, while explaining to the bewildered others just what this mysterious Meniere's Syndrome was all about. Everyone else did whatever they could to help. And, of course, Liz gave me her motel room, fed me (after I stopped throwing up), and offered me her wisdom about life's challenges.

Three years later, when I fell off my horse and landed in the hospital, goat folk banded together and held an online auction that raised thousands of dollars toward my medical bills. I would have liked to name each and every one of those kind souls, but many of them donated anonymously. Besides, there are so many good-hearted goat folk always helping each other out, I could never name them all.

Take the story of Mikey. One day in 1996, I received a phone call from a goat person asking me to post on the internet the sad tale of Mikey, the lost goat.

It seems that Mikey, a four month old LaMancha buckling was traveling eastward from Oregon to Utah with a load of Nubian-Boer bucks and does destined to become pack goats. He apparently grew tired of their company and escaped. He managed this feat while traveling at 40 miles per hour in the back of a truck going over a mountain pass in eastern Oregon. The door of the truck canopy came unlocked, probably from the jostling of those 150 pound Boer bucks, and Mikey rolled out. (Or else he unlocked the door himself and jumped; who's to say?)

A lady traveling some distance behind the truck noticed a small black goat with a bright red collar standing alongside the road. When she caught up with the truck full of goats, she waved the driver to pull over and asked if he was missing a small black one. He looked and saw that he was, thanked her, and backtracked to where Mikey was last seen. Although he searched high and low, Mikey had disappeared.

The distraught goat owner stopped at the next town and called the humane society. He also called Kathy Greysmith (the former owner of the Boer crosses), who called me. I posted the message on the Internet.

People from far and wide joined in the search. Linda Beal, Nubian breeder near Burns, Oregon, and a friend of Kathy's, drove up and down the highway. She also notified all the surrounding ranchers and area veterinarians. But she didn't hold out much hope for one little goat in an isolated area populated mostly by sagebrush and coyotes.

Miracles, we all learned, do happen. Two days later

a couple of women were hauling some sheep from western Oregon to the East side. Their route took them over that same road. There, alongside the road, was a small black goat with a red collar. The pair stopped. Mikey walked up to their pickup and jumped in. He was ready to go home.

Those kind souls inquired at the next town if anyone had lost a goat. The sheriff gave them the phone number of the Utah owner, who was overjoyed and amazed. He called Linda Beal who retrieved the little buck. As it turned out, the sheep people had relatives who would be driving from Oregon to Utah in a week and were willing to take Mikey with them.

Amazingly, the little buck arrived at his Utah home with only scratches and bruises to show for his adventure. Linda Beal theorized that a thunder and lightening storm the night Mikey was lost kept predators under cover rather than hunting for meals.

The fact that Mikey was found by good-hearted people who were in the right place at the right time shows that there are plenty of good folks in the world. And the number of people who helped search for Mikey shows that a lot of those good people raise goats.

I found them at the Oregon State Fair and, years later, on the internet and in my hospital room. Those crazy, wonderful goat folk are always there when you need them.

NUBIAN MOMENTS

Aging brings, I've learned, Senior Moments. Those are the moments when I can't remember where I put the hoof trimmers, what my buck's name is, or, some days, my own name.

My Nubians also have a brain problem, although it's not age related. They have what I call Nubian Moments. This is when they suddenly decide that the milk room they've been coming into calmly for six months is a very scary place and they flatly refuse to enter.

Some goats have far more Nubian Moments than others. Hopeless had, for quite some time, nothing but Nubian Moments. Her real name is Magic Hope. Her mother, Magic, has a lovely udder, flyaway ears and no brain. I had high hopes that Magic's daughter would inherit her mother's udder and her father's brain.

Half my hopes came true. I could tell before Hope freshened that she was building an udder to rival her mother's. I could also tell that, unfortunately, she had her mother's brain, or lack of it.

Since my kids nurse their dams, they are not bottle-kid friendly. However, after I start catching the mamas-to-be to put them on the milk stand for grain two months ahead of kidding, they soon become docile, cooperative yearlings. Most of them. Some take longer than others, but I have never had a goat that had to be run down and caught every single time she was supposed to come into the milk room — until Hope, who quickly became known as Hopeless.

This was not the usual moderately timid goat who hides in the middle of the herd and is relatively easy to corner. Oh no. Hopeless had full blown panic attacks, racing from side to side, banking off the walls, knocking over other goats and generally acting like the devil himself was after her. The other goats, fed up with her antics, bashed her in the ribs as she flew past as though to say, "Knock it off, you fruitcake! She just wants to feed you!"

It took an average of fifteen minutes a day to catch Hopeless and drag her screaming into the milk room as she flung herself into the air, onto the barn floor, upside down, sideways. There was simply no calming her down.

The first two weeks after this traumatic entry to the milk room she stood, quivering, unaware of the food beneath her nose. Finally one day she noticed that her mother, who was next to her on the double-headed milk stand, was eating something. She reached her head over and down and found . . . wonder of wonders, grain!

About every other day Hopeless rediscovered the grain. In between days she stood and quivered. By the time she freshened I was determined to sell her as soon as possible. She had, of course, a spectacularly beautiful doe kid and a lovely udder. Amazingly enough, she never objected to my milking her (after I'd run her down, caught her, and dragged her into the milk room.)

It was a month before Hopeless came into the milk room on her own. What changed her mind, I have no idea. I used the same procedure as always. Open the door, holler, "Come on, Hopeless!" in high hopes that she would actually come instead of racing to the far end of the barn. One morning, she picked her head up, looked at me, looked at the open door and calmly marched in and jumped on the milk stand.

From that day forth, she seemed to forget her fears and came into the milk room willingly, stood properly, ate politely, and let me milk. I went back to calling her Hope. She did not respond. She had been Hopeless for so long that Hope had no meaning to her.

Hope(less) still has her Nubian Moments. When we were gone for four days, she refused to enter the milk room for the farm sitter. I had told Bev not to worry, since all goats have kids nursing. If they had Nubian Moments, fine, let them be. On the last day, Hope decided she wanted that grain after all.

Once in a while, Hope still has panic attacks. Perhaps she turns a different way coming off the milk stand, or I don't take hold of her collar right away, or she sees something I don't. For whatever reason, or for no reason, she leaps into a full-blown Nubian Moment.

I have no intention of selling Hope. For one thing, I couldn't in good conscience stick anybody else with this neurotic animal. When she flips out, she really flips out.

I also can't sell her daughter. For one thing, I've yet to catch her. Brainlessness seems to worsen with each generation. I can't imagine what it will be like to try to get Hannah on the stand. She is a beautiful, insane mass of Nubian Moments.

"Why do you keep goats like that?" my husband asks.

"I dunno," I respond.

"What do you mean, you don't know?"

"Uh, gee, I dunno."

Another Senior Moment.

TECHNICOLOR GOATS

Now that I no longer show my goats and am no longer on milk test, I have different criteria for deciding which goats stay in the herd and which go. I used to keep two does of each age so I could fill the classes at the fair and maximize premiums. These does obviously had to be built well enough to place high, plus milk well enough to make decent test records.

My "keepers" still need to be built well enough to live a long time without problems and to milk well enough to be useful; but they don't have to be in different age groups. They do, however, need to have personalities that get along with mine.

In the past, I could put up with a screamer if she were drop-dead gorgeous and milky. Not any more. Likewise the airheads were tolerated if they could win their class and fill the bucket. No longer. (There are, of course, exceptions. Hopeless is still here.)

I prefer goats that are sensible and quiet (relatively speaking — they are Nubians, after all) plus milky and pretty. "Pretty," I'm embarrassed to admit, seems to have moved way up on the list of priorities.

There is a practical reason for this bias. When we go away and must hire farm-sitters, they have to know which goats to milk. For a few years, all my goats were brown. My farm-sitter complained bitterly that she couldn't tell the goats apart.

"But they wear numbered collars!" I protested.

"They wear them until you leave, then they lose them. Deliberately, I'm sure."

I suspect she was right.

The goats also wore numbered collars so the monthly tester could identify them. Now that I'm off test, most of the collars are languishing in a drawer. After all, I know my goats.

But the farm-sitter doesn't. Fortunately, the goats are no longer all brown. Slowly but surely, fanciful colors have been creeping into my herd.

Phantom probably started it all with her blue roan coat and multicolored children. Then there was the spotted buck who added designs to his offspring.

As I made up the list of milkers for the farm-sitter one day in 1997, for our first vacation in two years, I found myself describing the goats by color. There were hardly two alike!

There was the black with brown frosting, the black with white ears, the black with white splash, the red roan that's nearly white and the red roan with a white splash. Then there was the blue roan (Phantom), and the plain brown doe (the only one). There was the doe with a beard, the only one since Nubian does don't usually grow beards; and the doe with long teats. (Okay, so beards and teats aren't color distinctions. Nevertheless, they're distinctive.) Only three does were similar enough to need numbered collars.

After years of being color blind, of mocking breeders who paid the slightest attention to color when making breeding or keeping decisions, I became a convert. My goal for the future was to have a herd of does so unique from each other that anyone could tell them apart by color alone. I would call them the Fink Family Farm Amazing Technicolor Dream Goats.

I began saving kids by color. The boldly black-and-white spotted kid stayed. The red-with-white spotted kid was sold. (I already had a red with white spots.)

There were, however, exceptions. A plain brown kid stayed even though I already had a plain brown. This kid was the first doeling Diedra ever gave me. Diedra, red with white spots, was then seven and probably the best doe in my barn. I wouldn't care if her kid were bald, I wasn't about to sell her.

Now that her kid is a two-year-old milker, I'm reconsidering, even though Diedra still has not given me another doeling. Debutante is not the goat her mother is. But beauty skips a generation so I'm waiting to see how *her* kid turns out. Presuming Debutante ever gives me a doe kid.

I used to keep all the doe kids until they freshened so I could compare their udders and milk production. No longer. They all have reasonably good udders and enough milk. What they differ in is *color.*

Ergo, the red kid with the bold white splashes stays, the black with brown frosting goes . . . although I really love black with brown frosting. Maybe if one doe has a mostly brown head and one a mostly black head, they can both stay. I don't want to be rigid about this color thing.

It is great fun to look out in the pasture and see this swarm of color milling about. And to think how many years I ignored color! I may as well have been raising Toggs or Saanens or Oberhasli. If you have a colorful breed, why not flaunt it?

What's that you say? It's immoral to breed for color in a dairy breed? I used to say that, too, until I realized that you don't have to breed for color in order to get it. Color happens. I'm just selecting for variety of markings, all else being equal.

Two years after my conversion, Fink Family Farm Technicolor Dream Goats were a reality. White with tan splashes; heads with white, brown and black stripes; bizarre colors; wild designs. A visitor noticed that one doe had a rubber ducky on her side. It's true. The splash of white on a red doe is in the very distinct shape of a rubber ducky.

Yes, indeedy: unique and/or beautiful, we now have a herd of Fink Family Farm Amazing Technicolor Dream Goats.

PART III

SEASONAL
and other SAGAS

BLACK GOLD

Spring! When baby goats leap and frolic and the manure pile reaches the loafing-shed roof. When mothers-to-be wait calmly in their freshly cleaned kidding pens for nature to take its course. If nature takes more than a day, I have to clean the pen again. Then after the babies are born, I clean it some more.

Kidding season is manure season. Every day I clean out the main part of the barn and haul wheelbarrow after wheelbarrow load of that most abundant of all goat products to the back pasture. There I create new manure piles, farther from the roof.

In spite of these gallant efforts, the manure pack behind the barn under the loafing shed keeps growing. That's because I can't convince my goats to walk out to the back pasture to poop.

When visitors come to admire the frolicking baby goats in the spring, do they remark on my clean barn floor, neatly covered with golden-white straw? No. They talk about the manure pack just behind the barn.

"What are you going to do with all this *!@%?"

"We'll spread it on the pastures this summer, when the fields are dry enough."

"By this summer you won't be able to get out of the barn."

Some people are more appreciative of the gunk behind my barn. Town friends came one day to gather manure for their garden. They were thrilled with the well-composted stuff I gave them. It did not come from under the loafing shed, though. That stuff is like concrete.

No, the compost is in heaps in the back pasture where I and my trusty wheelbarrow pile the manure and straw. After a year or two, the mixture turns into a rich black compost. I use it for all my greenhouse potting needs.

After my friends left, I started thinking about this black gold I take for granted. Why not sell it? I could package the compost in plastic feed sacks — goodness knows I have enough of them — and take it to area garden stores. My compost isn't sterile, of course. But I figure, like worms in broccoli, weeds just prove the product is safe.

I'd have to sell manure for a pretty high price to pay for my labor. Not to mention feed costs. The expensive material that goes in one end of my goats comes out either the bottom spigots or the back hole. We all know the value of the bottom spigot stuff. What I've been neglecting is the back hole.

Town folks should be willing to pay dearly for back hole black gold. That's what I could label it — Black Gold. "Use Black Gold to make your garden produce a fortune."

I have the slogan, now all I need is the product bagged and distributed. Trouble is (besides a lack of energy after all this barn cleaning) I use every bit of Black Gold produced for my own garden and greenhouse.

The hard-packed manure under the loafing shed fertilizes the pastures (when the pastures are dry enough and we have a loader available and the tractor and manure spreader are functioning — all on the very same day). The looser manure that I've dumped in piles in the back field composts over time, then fertilizes my greenhouse plants.

The composted black gold is hauled by heavy wheelbarrow loads to the greenhouse, where I shovel the stuff onto a big screen-wire contraption draped over a large tub. I rub the compost back and forth until rocks and hard clumps are all that's left on top, with fine soil in the tub below. The soil, mixed with river sand, makes wonderful potting soil for tomato and other vegetable starts, house plants and exotic greenhouse flowers. It truly is black gold.

No, I can't sell my black gold. What I need to do instead is convince more people to produce their own black gold by buying some of my goats. They'll get their compost and I'll have fewer goats eating expensive food and then depositing it in smelly pellets under the loafing shed. Or in the kidding pens.

Kidding pen manure doesn't go on the back field piles. It goes to next year's garden, which is this year's chicken pen. We rotate chickens and garden each year. Manure management around here is rather complicated. I've tried to explain this to Johnny when he helps clean. He just glares at me and says, "Just tell me where you want this *!@%."

Ah, spring on the farm. What a glorious time. A time for crocuses, daffodils, kid goats and, more than anything else, that four-letter word — manure.

THE WHEELBARROW YEARS

Every year has a special flavor in our goat barn. Some years are Feeder Kid Years. That's when all the kids decide to live inside the hay feeders. Kids go in and out of the feeders every year, but once in a while, they spend most of their time in there and I spend most of my time throwing them out.

Then there's the Early Kid year. That's when all the does decide to freshen before they're due, dropping their kids outside the kidding pens. This is often the same year as the Stolen Kids Phenomenon. Greedy mothers steal other kids before the true mother notices she's had any.

Some years are the Years of the Tightrope Kids. The kids spend their days climbing about on window ledges and other impossible places. We've had years when the kids spent all their time walking about on the backs of their mothers. (Kids and moms live together on our farm.) And years when they spent their time finding holes in the fences and cavorting where they shouldn't be.

Sometimes, we have the most annoying of all — The Years of the Wheelbarrow Kids.

I clean the milker's side of the barn every day with a wheelbarrow, then haul the manure and straw outside.

Kids love to play in wheelbarrows. In a normal year, rambunctious kids occasionally knock over my wheelbarrow when it is partly full. This frightens the entire herd who go racing out of the barn in terror. Sometimes.

Some years are different. I don't know if it's the position of the planets or my attitude, but some years the kids don't wait until I'm on the far side of the barn, or until I have left for a minute to tend to some calamity outside the milkers' area. They hardly wait until I have the wheelbarrow inside the barn before they begin leaping in and out. No matter how many times I shoosh them away, they keep coming back.

Nothing gives these kids greater glee than pushing off as they jump out of the manure-filled wheelbarrow, sending it toppling sideways, spilling its load. In those years, the does grow so accustomed to my crashing wheelbarrow that, far from fleeing in terror, they don't even take their heads out of the manger.

After the third time I reshovel a load of manure into a toppled wheelbarrow, I vow to sell all the kids in the barn or eat them. Their antics are no longer cute.

But I must admit I laughed one day when a kid took a flying leap into the as-yet-empty wheelbarrow and landed half in and half out, rocking back and forth on her belly. She kicked frantically, leaned backwards, and succeeded in jumping out of the way as the wheelbarrow fell over on its side.

Did this teach her a lesson? Hardly. I had no more than righted the barrow when she was back again, dancing in circles inside her tinny stage.

What I need is an old wheelbarrow to embed in concrete in the barnyard so the kids čan play without driving me nuts. Although they probably won't think it nearly as much fun if their toy refuses to fall over.

A friend suggested I put a decoy barrow in the barnyard for the kids to play in while I load mine. I may try that but I suspect the attraction will fade quickly, because what kids really love is playing king of the ever-growing mountain as I load the barrow with manure.

It is amazing how high kids can jump. At some point, they bounce off the side of the growing mound instead of landing on top which, naturally, knocks the wheelbarrow over. I then must re-shovel all the manure.

When we build the new barn (the one we've been talking about for ten years), I plan to have wonderful nesting areas and hidey holes for kid goats so they won't even think about climbing into hay feeders. They'll have a playground filled with goat toys: rock mountains, old wheelbarrows, teeter totters, balance beams, trees to climb — everything a rambunctious, capricious caprine could want.

Then the kids will never again knock over my wheelbarrow. Instead, every year will be the Year of the Cute Kids Playing on Their Playground Toys.

Well, I can dream, can't I?

FENCE TESTING

Goats are great fence testers. They will find any weakness, any crevice, any gate not securely latched. But when D-Ann landed inside a tiny area bounded by four-foot welded wire fence panels, I couldn't figure how she got there. Or why.

There was lots of grass in the goat pasture. Granted, the tiny area had taller grass because the panel holes are too small for heads. It was securely fenced a few years ago for a tree that was to grow and provide shade for the animals. The tree died but the enclosure remained.

Impenetrable though the enclosure seemed to be, inside it was D-Ann, screaming her head off. I called Johnny to help me lift her out because I couldn't figure any other way. He kept muttering, "But this is the only place on the farm goats can't get to. How'd she do it?"

If anything had frightened her enough to jump, this is not the direction she would have jumped. The enclosure is in the middle of a field. She could have run any direction. There was no earthly reason for her to be where she was.

"Maybe aliens dropped her in," I suggested.

D-Ann is only two years old, so we didn't completely break our backs throwing her over the fence. But it wasn't easy. Still muttering, Johnny kept tugging at the solid fencing to see if there was any way she could have . . . And then he found it.

One end of the panel abutted a sturdy wood fence

post, but the staples that had attached it to the post were gone. Still inside the enclosure, we pulled the fence toward us, reconstructing the gap D-Ann must have created that let her push her way in. The fence panel, being stiff, popped back into place after she passed through, and she couldn't get out. Nor could we discover the problem when we pushed against the fence from the inside.

That still doesn't answer the question as to why she bothered to push her way in when she has acres of grass at her disposal. But she's a goat, and goats, I guess, just have to test fences.

In the woven wire fences around the barn paddocks, our guardian dogs have spread the wires to make holes big enough to crawl through. Once a young goat finds one of those holes, the rest of the herd soon works at enlarging it until they, too, escape. Usually into the pond area, which is gated away from the garden. (After enough years living with goats one learns to have multiple fences between goat quarters and garden.)

One spring day I found the entire herd happily devouring wild roses and blackberries around the pond — which was fine — and water iris and bamboo — which wasn't. After chasing the brats back into their pasture, I used the bamboo canes I'd recently cut from our bamboo groves to weave a patch over the escape hole. When I checked them later that day, the miserable creatures were out again. They'd pushed aside my bamboo fix and were clear-cutting once more. I added more bamboo canes.

Immediately, the entire herd stormed the fence and began rubbing against the bamboo poles, putting their heads through the wire and pushing it, chewing on the bamboo and even the wire (I'm not kidding) and working bamboo and fencewire every direction possible. That bamboo stockade held firm for several months before the next break-out. I added more bamboo.

The price of freedom is eternal vigilance, as goats well know; and so they keep testing the fence until they find a way out yet again and I keep fixing holes, trying to keep them in. Even if there's less grass on the other side of the fence, goats will try to get there, just because it's the other side of the fence. It's a matter of pride, I think.

Other animals on this farm test fences, too, but none so persistently and cleverly as goats. I think fences are considered a challenge in the goat world. I can just hear two yearlings egging each other on: "Hey, bet you can't clear that fence, lard butt."

"Who you calling lard butt, double-chin? Let's see you jump it."

At which point they start chasing each other around the pasture, building up speed until they either sail over the fence or run into it. Or get hung up halfway over — because Nubians are actually not very good jumpers.

Nubians are great at pushing through things, though, with their massive bodies and bull heads. One of their best tricks is rubbing against metal fence posts until they bend them, then walking the woven wire fence down until they're on the other side. Once their weight is off the fence, it springs back and they can't return to their pasture. So, after devouring whatever is out there that they shouldn't, they stand baaing sorrowfully (and loudly) begging to get back in, or else they run up and down the fence line screaming.

D-Ann was baaing sorrowfully and loudly because there wasn't enough room to run in the little place she found herself. Maybe it wasn't the grass she was after. Maybe she was just testing to see if we could figure out how she got in there. Now that the herd knows how dumb we are (we didn't discover D-Ann's route of entry until after we'd nearly dislocated our backs throwing her over the fence), they'll probably work the fences even harder.

It's a good thing I have a lot of bamboo canes.

THE CASE OF THE DISAP-
PEARING GOATS

It happened soon after I listened to a radio rebroad-cast about Chupacabra. Chupacabra means "goat sucker" and was a creature supposedly attacking goats and other livestock in Mexico. Eyewitness reports were of a bizarre creature with scales and feathers that stood on its hind legs and had red eyes.

The radio rerun also talked about alien abductions and other topics a bit beyond the edge of my credibility. "Imagine people believing that stuff," I thought.

Then it happened. I went out to do chores that July evening only to find one of Connie's new babies missing. Just the day before, I had turned Connie and her twins out of the kidding pen, where they had lived for the three days since Connie's blessed event.

"Probably hiding somewhere," I mused. I checked the usual kid hiding places — under feeders, in feeders, under the barn, in the concrete culverts that are used as goat toys in the pasture — but did not find the missing kid. When I brought Connie onto the milk stand, one side of her udder was full. The kid had not nursed for quite some time.

I started to worry. Before darkness descended, I searched the pasture. The guardian dogs were not upset. When I asked them "Where's the baby?" they didn't take me to any sleeping kid goat. The grass was very tall and it would not have been possible to search through all of it, but I felt sure the dogs would have led me to a kid if one were out there.

Connie, being a yearling, didn't yet know how to count and so was not disturbed by having only one child. I finally gave up and went to bed, hoping that the baby would come out of hiding by the next morning.

It did not. I finished chores and renewed my search. I shone a light under every corner of the barn, walked the field again, asked the dogs again. Something must have taken it, I now felt sure. But the dogs did not act as though anything foreign had been on the place. It must have been something from the air — a large hawk or owl, although no hawk or owl had ever bothered our baby goats before, and usually the dogs bark ferociously when any come near.

In sadness, I returned to the house.

Later that afternoon I heard a wee kid bleating pitifully from the field. I ran outside. It was Connie's missing buckling! He was standing fifty yards behind the barn, crying toward the herd which was at the very end of a 2 1/2 acre field. They ignored him.

I called the goats and they came running — right past me and the forlorn baby and into the barn. I carried the baby to his mother who sniffed him as he dove for her udder. "Oh, yeah, you're mine, too, aren't you? I forgot about you. Where ya been, kid?"

Since he had his mouth full, I answered for him, "Hunkered in the grass, waiting for you," I told her. "Why didn't you keep him with you?"

That night I went out to do chores with not a worry on my mind since Connie's kid had been found. I counted noses and discovered to my dismay that the same tan kid with the white splash on his side was gone again! Not only that, but two of Celia's three kids, two weeks old, were also missing.

Celia, being older and smarter than Connie, was standing at the back of the barn, looking toward the pasture, crying. She had only one lonesome baby by her side.

I took the flashlight and scoured the fields. Surely I could find three kids nestled together. I looked under the barn. Near the far side, movement was visible between floor joists and dirt. Was it baby goats?

Nope, a large rat.

Where were my babies? Could this be the work of Chupacabra? Had the infamous Goat Sucker of Mexico moved north? Surely the dogs would have barked.

Alien abduction? Hmm, possibly. Aliens might have beamed the kids up to do tests on them, as the people interviewed on that radio program asserted had been done to them. When the experiments were concluded, the aliens would return my three baby goats, just as they had returned the one. (It's amazing how quickly our minds accept, when baffled, explanations that were previously unthinkable.)

The next morning, Celia was still crying at the back of the barn. I looked where she was looking, and there, one hundred yards out, were two small black goats, barely visible above the tall grass. Hooray! They were back! Where there were two, there surely must be three. I walked to the kids, Celia following cautiously. There was no other baby to be seen.

Celia led her children back to the barn, talking to them the entire way. "Don't you ever give me a scare like that again! Where have you been?! I've been worried sick."

Connie's baby just had to be nearby. Perhaps it was in the old equipment rusting in the field. I had checked there before, but maybe I missed something.

Sure enough, behind a wheel of the old, decrepit manure spreader, lay a baby goat, watching me as I approached. The grass was beat down next to him as though two other babies had been there until recently. Likely they heard their mother calling and tried to find their way through the high grass to the sound of her voice. Since Connie wasn't crying, her baby stayed put.

Apparently, the babies had followed their mothers out to the field instead of staying by the barn with an old grandma goat. I had stopped feeding alfalfa in the morning because there was so much grass and browse to be eaten in the fields. The goats were fed hay at night only, and so the grandma goats, who usually stayed in to baby-sit and munch hay, were going out with the herd. That left no one to baby-sit at the barn, so the kids tagged along with their mothers.

When the youngsters grew tired, they lay down and took a nap. The herd continued to graze, moving away from the nap spot. When the kids woke up, the herd was gone. Not being able to see over the tall grass, they stayed where they were until the herd happened to graze past them again. At least, that's my conjecture. Why my dogs didn't lead me to the babies is a question I asked them but they just wagged their tails and slobbered.

That very day, I mowed the fields. I also started feeding hay again in the mornings. No baby goats disappeared after the grass was cut, although the grandmas did not stay by the barn. Those green fields were just too lush to ignore.

Tall grass is not so exciting a reason for disappearing baby goats as is alien abductions, but it is certainly easier to correct. (And not as gruesome as a blood-sucking, goat-eating Chupacabra.) Of course, I've no proof of what happened. It could have been aliens. If so, they either completed their experiments or grew tired of being sucked on by hungry baby goats.

HAY HAULING AND COM-
PLAINING

Every summer when we haul hay, I decide to cut down on goats. Haying has always been hard work, but the older I get, the harder it seems. Worse yet, nobody sympathizes with me anymore. I guess they've heard my complaints too many times. And they've noticed that, in spite of my yearly vows to have fewer mouths to feed, I don't.

We always haul hay during the hottest weeks of the year. It has been pointed out to me that hay isn't ready until the weather turns hot; therefore I should be thankful for hot weather because without it, I wouldn't get any hay. And why didn't we haul during the wee hours of the morning and the late evening?

We do. But, as the years have passed, our wee hours have grown a wee bit later and our late evenings earlier. And the hay bales heavier. And my back weaker. But I am thankful. Thankful I can still get up the next morning.

Every year I vow to hire someone to deliver hay to my barn and put it in for me. But that costs money and I'm cheap. So Johnny and I do it ourselves.

"If we take it slow, it won't be bad," Johnny assures me. Well, we take it slow (there's no other way I can take it) and... it's bad.

"We were hauling hay all last week during that 90

degree weather," I told a friend. "It was awful."

"Hah! You don't know what awful is until you've moved irrigation pipe," she countered. "You're hot and sticky, the children are grumbling over having to help, and there are bees buzzing all around your head. You can't do anything about them because both hands are carrying heavy pipe. Then you trudge half a mile down to start the irrigation pump and it doesn't work. So you have to take (something) apart (I forgot what she took apart) and fish the snail out."

The tale went on, but I wasn't paying attention, since I was looking around for someone who might listen to my complaints and cluck sympathetically.

"Why don't you sell some goats?" the new listener suggested, after clucking sympathetically. "Then you wouldn't have to put up so much hay."

How original. Johnny suggests that every year. Actually, that's what I am determined to do this year. Just as I was determined to cut down last year. And the year before that.

Bucking hay is a little like child birth. After it's over, you forget the pain and the joy kicks in. The joy is having a barn full of sweet-smelling hay, or in our case, three barns full.

On the first day of bucking hay, there's anticipation and a little anxiety. I'm glad the hay is ready, since we're almost out, but I worry that Johnny will start talking about too many animals to feed.

After the first ten tons, I'm just hoping I can hold out to the end. After twenty tons, I'm considering selling goats and sheep and cattle and changing jobs.

"But what would you rather be doing?" asks Johnny. He gets his second wind after the fourth load or so, about the time I'm thinking about selling the farm.

"What a life!" he extols. "Fresh air; beautiful scenery; good, honest physical labor. And think of the delicious food we eat because of this hay. Would you rather be in an RV, traveling around the country?"

"No," I admit, "that would be awful. No flower beds,

no baby goats to cuddle, no fresh vegetables from the garden. Just campgrounds with other RVs right next to you." At least, that's what I say when he asks after ten tons.

After twenty tons, I say, "No schedule, no backbreaking work, nothing to do but hike the countryside and look at wildflowers that don't need weeding. Suppose anyone would trade us an RV for a herd of goats?"

But once the hay is in the barn, my attitude changes. The blisters heal, the milk-raised beef and pork tastes so good, and the energy level returns . . . eventually. I forget about cutting down on livestock. However, to make the experience truly worthwhile, I need to complain.

One year, having exhausted all my local friends, I complained on a goat-oriented e-mail list on the Internet. That was a big mistake. The Net is world wide.

"You're complaining? Try loading hay in Florida's heat and humidity."

Then I heard from Kansas, South Africa and Tasmania.

"Only 90 degrees F? How do you stay warm?"

I learned about a lot of places I don't need to visit during summertime if we ever sell the farm and buy an RV. But at least on the e-mail list nobody suggested I raise fewer goats. They're all in it as deep as I am.

TEST DAY BLUES

Looking back to the days when I was still on milk production testing, I wonder why I didn't quit sooner. Here is a column I wrote in August of 1989.

Since I leave babies on their moms, my tester calls 12 hours before arriving to tell me to lock the little darlings up. Usually, I lock up a doe's kids while their mother is on the milk stand so I don't miss any of the little monsters. Alas, this time, I just grabbed babies and pitched them into the holding pen. When I couldn't find any more, except the two who are on a nurse goat, I quit.

I checked several times to make sure, but with sixteen milkers milling about, calling for their young ones, I could only see one kid at a time. There was brown Nene (pronounced naynay), and beige Zee Zee. Wherever I looked, only Nene and Zee Zee could be seen.

In another area of the barn, the little doeling with the broken leg is quartered separately with her two siblings and Phoebe, their dam, in a double pen with connecting paddock. I closed the gate to one of the pens, leaving Phoebe on one side, her babies on the other. Then I went to the house, confident all was well.

How wrong I was.

The next morning, the tester, Bev, and I strode to the barn. The first thing we noticed was little Broken-Leg cavorting (as well as a goat with a splint on its leg can cavort) in the paddock with her brother, sister . . . and mother! The kids all looked full and happy. They should have: Phoebe's udder was empty.

I groaned. Bev snickered. (She has a warped sense of humor.) The barn sheets have no place to indicate that kids broke out of their pen and sucked their dam dry, so the tester used the closest equivalent she could find: "Spilled milk."

Oh well. Phoebe is just one out of sixteen milkers. The others would still have accurate tests. Or so I thought. Cha Cha came in. Cha Cha is a heavy milker. I babbled merrily to Bev as I milked, gossiping about this and that. The bucket was two-thirds full when I stopped milking to make a picture of something with my hands — I don't remember what, but I find it difficult to talk without using my hands. Cha Cha must have thought I was through milking. She picked her back end off the ground and set it to one side, knocking the milk pail over. A white waterfall cascaded off the milk stand, flooding the milk room.

"Oh, no!"

Another "spilled milk" — this time genuinely "spilled".

As I mournfully swept Cha Cha's milk down the drain, I heard little choking noises coming from my tester's corner. She had her back to me, but her shoulders were shaking in a suspicious manner.

"It's not funny!" I growled.

"I know," she managed to sputter between suppressed giggles, "but I can't help it." And she continued choking on her chuckles.

I milked the other does in stony silence, keeping my hands on the teats where they belonged. Until yearling Sondra arrived. Then I let loose with a scream. Sondra's udder was empty.

"What happened?!" I bellowed. "I know there were no kids left except Deedee's twins." (Thirteen-year-old Deedee is the nurse goat.) I stomped out to the milkers' area . . . and there were two Nene's, standing side by side. One of them was Susie, Sondra's doeling. Susie looks just like Nene.

Another "spilled milk."

"I thought Susie was Nene," I explained to Bev. "And Nene is supposed to be in there, with Zee Zee. Nene and Zee Zee are sisters. But Susie isn't supposed to be in there because she isn't Deedee's; she's Sondra's. She just looks like Deedee's," I babbled. "I mean she looks like Nene."

Now Bev was guffawing instead of giggling. "Someone asked me just yesterday," she gasped, between heehaws, "why I test goats. I couldn't think of an answer. Now I know. This is better than a situation comedy on television." And off she went again in gales of laughter.

Somehow, I failed to see the humor of the situation.

"Three lactation records ruined in one day," I muttered. "This must be a new high . . . or low."

But they weren't completely ruined. The computer compensated somewhat after reading the evening milk weights, when I successfully kept all kids locked away from their dams.

"Next month," I told my sniggering tester, "most of these kids will be weaned, so test day should be less eventful."

Bev looked disappointed.

CLEANING
THE MILK ROOM

One day in the fall of 1997, I found the milk room. It wasn't lost, really, just hidden beneath a ton of clutter, cobwebs and filth. I had been meaning to resurrect it all summer, but something always came up.

I think the turning point came when I could not see the ducks that landed on our pond. The milk room windows look out on the pond. Or they do when you can see through them, which I couldn't.

Cleaning the windows, however, necessitates removing all the stuff from the counter beneath them. It's amazing how much junk I can accumulate: calf bottles and nipples, syringes, collars, broken collars, medications, milk buckets, empty containers of various descriptions and purposes, lists, paper towels, notes, clippers, used A-I pipettes and more.

There was even a squirt gun that I used on an obnoxious buck a few times. The gun was broken and the buck in the freezer. Who knows why I hadn't thrown it away.

Although I'd long intended to spruce up the place, I never seemed to have time to make a special trip to the barn to clean. But one evening, when Johnny was feeding hay and water and my goats were taking a long time eating their grain, I had free time between goat milkings. I couldn't stare out the window at what was on the pond because the window was too dirty, so I started to sort the counter. The more I sorted and put away and threw away, the more enthused I became about the project.

Soon I was working in a veritable frenzy, milking two goats as quickly as I could, then sorting while they finished their grain. By the time the last of the eleven milkers had come and gone, the counter was clear except for the stuff that lives there full time.

Then I realized with horror the extent of the filth on the counter. It's funny how you can live in a disaster zone and never notice until something, like being unable to identify the bird that just landed on your pond because you can't see through the muck on the window, opens your eyes and you find yourself mortified by the mess.

For the next week, every evening milking was interspersed with scrubbing and vacuuming and washing. (Well, the vacuuming was done during the day, without goats. Scrubbing they can handle. The vacuum would dry them up.)

Johnny was impressed with my zeal.

"I'm impressed with your zeal," he said. "But are you remembering that we have company arriving tomorrow?"

"So?"

"Well, the milk room looks very nice but the house is a mess."

"I can't see the pond from the house."

"Huh?"

"I can't see the pond from the house, so I didn't notice the house windows are dirty."

"They're not, particularly. But the rest of the house is."

I'd been meaning to clean the house all summer, too. We do a quick run through when company is due but never quite get around to really cleaning. We'd had company all summer that year. (We usually do.) My theory is summer company will spend more time in the barn than in the house so the barn should be clean. And it generally is, except for the milk room.

But summer was about over. Autumn company spends more time in the house than the barn. The house was a mess. But the milk room sparkled! (Relatively speaking.) Perhaps I could entertain in the milk room?

I couldn't bear any more major cleaning projects right then: the milk room filled my quota for the year. Just washing the windows was a project of epic proportions. It's not that they're big; it's just that they're, well, difficult. The original panes blew out so many times in storms that Johnny became fed up and nailed another pane of glass in front of them as a buffer.

Spiders decided that the space between the two sets of windows was created just for them. It is not possible to employ my usual broom technique to the cobwebs on these windows. The broom won't fit between the two layers. So I took a vacuum with a long skinny tube to suck the cobwebs out. It didn't work. Cobwebs are tough. Plus there's no way to scrub between the layers.

The only solution is to take out the pane of glass, which is nailed into place with slats of wood. Knowing that I would surely break the glass, I enlisted Johnny's help. As long as he had to take it out, I suggested he wash it while I did other things, since he'd have to help nail it back in place anyway: the barn has shifted and the pane doesn't fit.

Neither does anything else. As the barn settles farther and farther into the dirt, the doors no longer shut, the cabinets are parting company with their hinges, and the window panes periodically burst under the tension. One pane of the original windows is gone completely. A second pane rests askew.

Two cabinet doors have fallen off and have not been replaced. The floor and ceiling no longer meet the walls and crud fills every gap. Someday, we're going to build a new barn, hopefully before this one collapses in on itself.

Cleaning our milk room is definitely not for the faint of heart. But clean it was, for a while that year, thanks to my Herculean efforts. And Johnny's. He did a great job on the windows.

In time (not much time, at that) the spiders returned, as did the dust and the junk on the counter. Any day now, I'll become inspired to clean again. Probably the next time a duck lands on the pond that I can't identify because I can't see out the windows.

LUSTY VOICES

In the fall of 1997, I discovered why I used to breed my does the first time they came into heat. To shut them up.

Thanks to my uncertain health of the previous two years, I had let some does milk through without rebreeding. That fall those does decided enough was enough. Whenever they came into heat, they raised the rafters on the barn and rattled the windows.

The other does were almost as noisy, probably for fear I'd leave them kidless, too. That fall the does all synchronized their screaming heats. I swear every doe in the barn came in on the very same day in November. The day we had out-of-town, citified, company.

I knew there'd be trouble when this city family walked into my house and the children asked, "Where's your television?"

"We don't have one," I responded.

"You don't have a *TV*??" exclaimed the incredulous kids. "What do you *do*?"

"Let's go to the barn and you'll find out," I foolishly suggested. As we neared, the noise intensified.

"Linda," asked the mother of the TV addicts. "What's wrong with your goats? Are they in pain?"

"No, they're Nubians."

"You're sure they're not in pain?"

"I'm sure. They're just hor . . . um, I mean, they would like to be bred to the bucks."

"Oh, my. I didn't know goats were . . . like that."

I was tempted to say, "Oh, not all are. But mine are really into sex. I should probably start limiting how much television they watch." But, of course, I didn't.

I stopped taking people to the barn that fall. In fact, I kept them as far away as possible. Even though I had given in and bred some of the does, there were still quite a few coming into heat and shrieking every 18 days or so.

I knew I would have to wean the yearling does sooner or later. They were as big as their dams. The noise then would be non-stop. I considered leaving town for a month or so.

I honestly didn't realize that Nubians could be that noisy, although I'd raised Nubians for over twenty-five years. In the past, as soon as they bawled I threw them in with a buck (or on the stand to be bred artificially.) There was only one noisy heat period per year per goat. Since some does start coming into heat in July, others in August, others in September or October, my kid crop was nicely spaced out. And so was the noise.

But that year I was the one who was spaced out from all the racket in the barn.

The bucks were surprisingly calm about the commotion, probably because they each had live-in girlfriends. My bucks seem much calmer and happier (not to mention quieter) when they live with does, so I keep dry yearlings or older does that have dried up for one reason or another with the bucks they've been bred to.

This can have surprising results. Toward the end of the noisy 1997 November, I moved some of the obviously pregnant yearlings out of the buck pen so I could move a couple screaming, sex-starved does in. As I lifted the very large yearlings onto the milk stand for long overdue foot trimming, I noticed that they had rather well-developed udders. I checked the calendar and realized that their first possible due date was December 4, only one week hence.

Somehow, in my misguided attempts to keep the bucks happy yet not breed too many goats, I had managed to create a nearly year-long kidding season — starting in December and ending five months after I gave up and threw the last screaming doe in with a buck.

There are quackless ducks in the world, why aren't there baa-less goats? Do other breeds vocalize their lust the way Nubians do? Or is it just *my* Nubians?

These were questions I pondered as the sounds from the barn ricocheted off my eardrums. (I couldn't think about anything more profound with all that racket.)

Since then I have limited the number of does screaming all breeding season by only letting a few does each year milk through without rebreeding. Like terms of office on a school board, the two-year lactations are staggered. Every three weeks a doe or two screams for sex, but the volume is considerably lower than that fateful fall of 1997, when the entire herd raised their voices in lustful cacophony.

OUT OF THE GUTTER

Western Oregon is wet in the winter. Some years are wetter than others. One particularly wet November we had 24 inches of rain. Little pools of water appeared with every footstep or hoof print in the pasture. A lake formed behind the goat barn.

One stormy morning late that November, I was wheeling my load of manure out of the barn through the wall of water that poured out of the rusted-through gutters, or what was left of them, when something snapped inside me. I suddenly knew that I could not live another winter with a swimming pool behind the barn.

Perhaps if goats liked to swim, I would have felt differently. But they don't. Nor do they appreciate mud. Neither do I. I hate it. The goats refuse to go through it, but I don't have a choice. Yet . . . we always have choices, right? Mine was to fix the gutters.

The reason the real handyman of the family hadn't fixed the barn gutters was because they were unfixable and (I thought) unreplaceable. They were obviously unfixable as they were completely rusted out in numerous places.

I thought they were not replaceable because, I remember being told, the wood they were fastened to was rotten, as was the wood that wood was fastened to, so there was no place to fasten new gutters. I would have to wait for the new barn before there could be new gutters. That very same barn that I'd been waiting on for ten years, that looked no closer to reality. There were too many other priorities.

So, I put down my wheelbarrow and headed for Johnny's shop. I pawed through piles of old gutters and downspouts, looking for gutters I could stick under the roof on top of the old ones, without having to take anything off or screw anything on.

My idea seemed simple enough. But, like everything else in life, it wasn't. The nail thingies holding up the old gutters kept me from pushing my replacement gutters down very far. So I stuffed them sideways under the edge of the roof. Some of the gutters I tried had too much lip to work, or old screws sticking out inconveniently, or any number of other problems.

Goats, by the way, do not like long gutters or ladders being carried through their barn. Every trip from the gutter cache saw goats flying in all directions, climbing walls, and otherwise trying to escape the long metal alligators that were about to devour them.

When I climbed the ladder with a gutter balanced precariously, the wind came up and threatened to take me and my gutter sailing. This, of course, set off a new frenzy of goat hysterics.

After jamming the new gutters into place through wind and driving rain, water still leaked out of the old ones. Making water flow where you want it is harder than it looks.

Next I cut an old rubber bath mat into strips (fortunately, I never throw anything away). I laid the strips in the bottom of the old gutters over the rusted-out portions. Still the water seeped under and out.

My downspout efforts were more successful. After a few dozen trips from the shop's miscellany piles, with the resulting goat stampedes, I found a downspout that would fit into the drainpipe below. The drainpipe hadn't been used for years. What was the point since little of the water made it to that end of the gutter?

I don't know how many different pipes and combinations thereof I tried before figuring out that the thingie poking out of the gutter could be pushed up, thereby making my downspout the right length after all, and then poked back down again, holding the downspout in place. (Johnny later told me it shouldn't have been pushable — that it must have rusted apart. Well, I'm glad it did or I never would have had my downspout.)

Since I was already drenched, I figured I may as well try to solve the gutter problem on another side of the barn, where water poured freely off the roof into the paddocks beyond the buck pens. I don't have to walk through that water wall as often, but the bucks do.

I had used up all available gutters that had any chance of fitting inside the rusted-out ones, so instead I laid long gutters across the fences dividing the buck pens, below the drips from the old gutters. Being long and wimpy, the "new" ones collapsed this way and that, dumping their rain water wherever.

Back to Johnny's piles I went to find heavy long pipes and lay them inside my gutters. Later that day the wind and rain returned with a vengeance. The pipe-held gutters stood firm, dumping their load of rain harmlessly into the pig pen beyond.

But two of the four gutter pieces overhanging the swimming pool behind the barn promptly blew off. Even so, most of the water went into the downspout instead of into the pool.

Excited by my success, such as it was, I decided to use pipes for the overhead gutters to keep them from blowing out . . . until I worried that heavy pipes high overhead would cause the whole jerry-rigged mess to fall down and kill a goat (or me). That night I confessed my sins to the real handyman and asked for advice.

Johnny laughed, then continued reading the paper.

"How can I keep the new gutters from blowing off?" I persisted. "I'm afraid pipes would pull the gutters off the barn."

"Well, you could try weighting them down with tires." Then he laughed some more and went back to his paper.

I could see he wasn't taking this seriously. Finally he admitted that he had new gutters to go up but hadn't had time to do it. The next day, I put pipes in the overhead gutters, rationalizing that the weight would be distributed over a long distance.

There was still water dripping into the former swimming pool, which I replaced with frequently overflowing buckets, but for the most part the water went down the drain. I felt enormously proud of myself.

However, I didn't linger when I walked under the edge of the roof. And I ducked when I went out of the buck pens. One night when Johnny was tending to the bucks' water tubs, he didn't duck.

I heard a horrendous THUD, then a loud exclamation of pain followed by numerous unprintable words. Johnny had run into my pipe-reinforced gutters.

"Did you knock them out of place?" I asked with concern.

Johnny didn't answer. He just kept holding his head and moaning. Not long after, Johnny spent a day taking down my contraptions and putting up new gutters.

It is wonderful to have a (relatively) dry barn yard. All the work I went to was worth the effort. It might have been years before Johnny put up new gutters if he hadn't cracked his head on mine.

WANTED:
SKILLED MILKER

The ability to milk goats is a valuable skill. Such a skill is good not just for impressing school children who tour our farm and take turns at milking, only to watch in awe when I finish up for them. Nor just for proving I can do one thing, at least, (somewhat) better than my spouse.

No, my skill as a hand milker could be critically important from a global perspective. I sell milk to the Oregon Wildlife Center, a ranch that raises endangered species of antelope and other ungulates in cooperation with several zoos. They are trying to develop breeding populations to someday reintroduce into the wild.

Nancy and Dick often hand-raise animals that are orphaned or whose mothers don't have enough milk or reject their offspring. They have learned through experience that none of the zoo-developed milk replacers work half so well as goat milk.

Since I am one of the few goat owners in this area crazy enough to milk year round, Nancy and Dick buy their milk from me. My milk has saved several Lesser Kudus, of which there are only about 45 in captivity in North America; several Mhorr Gazelles, which are extinct in the wild; and others.

One day in the fall of 1997, Nancy called in a state

of panic. Their yearling Speke's gazelle had freshened (or whatever gazelles do) for the first time and refused to have anything to do with her baby. Nancy stock-piles frozen colostrum from my goats, but in this case she wanted fresh. It was critical that this rare baby survive!

I had no goats recently fresh so I gave her the number of the nearest goat dairy, which wasn't very near. Soon Nancy called back. "We have to get milk down him soon. He's very weak. Could you come over here and try to milk out his mother?"

"Sure," I said.

The year before, I'd been asked to milk out a Lesser Kudu, but that mama turned out to have no milk. I didn't have much hope this time. Nancy told me that Speke's gazelles are very fragile and temperamental, the mothers often reject their offspring, and zoos have a very difficult time hand-raising the babies.

But I drove the twelve miles to Nancy's and told her I'd do my best. Nancy and a helper carefully herded the frightened young mother into the restraining device. The helper put a blanket over the gazelle's head, and Nancy and I slowly opened the back of the squeeze.

The tiny animal was maybe a foot and a half tall and could not have weighed more than thirty pounds.

"I didn't know gazelles came this small," I said to Nancy.

"Yeah, the Spekes are really tiny. And very frail."

Frail is right. The legs looked like long, crooked pencils. The udder seemed full of milk, but it was smaller than an orange and sucked right up to that little thing's belly. The teats were no bigger than my little fingernail.

When I reached gently under to touch the udder, the gazelle lay down. Nancy had to hold the poor, terrified thing's back-end up while I half-knelt, half-lay on the concrete floor and used the two-finger, first-freshener stripping technique to milk the miniature udder.

Actually, the orifices were surprisingly large and milked fairly easily. Nonetheless, each squirt only drew a tiny amount of milk. It took a long time crouched on that hard floor to milk each side.

"Nancy," I whispered (we were trying not to frighten the gazelle), "if you ever start raising endangered mice, I'm changing my phone number."

Before the second side was completely milked out, I made Nancy try, so she could milk the gazelle next milking. She was successful, but considerably slower than I.

"Wow, this is hard!" she whispered.

We then took our precious four ounces of gazelle colostrum to the house, where the baby was lying lethargically in a box. The three-pound gazelle mouthed the nipple, but couldn't figure out how to suck. I stroked under his tail (which stimulates the sucking reflex) while Nancy threw colostrum down the front end. Eventually, she got an ounce and a half of liquid in him, which we thought was pretty good. We didn't want to tube feed unless absolutely necessary.

Nancy put the little guy back in the box. Sammy, as she dubbed him, became the ninth male Speke's gazelle alive in North America. But he wasn't very alive.

As Nancy set Sammy gently down after the half hour feeding, he tried to stand, wobbling dangerously on his toothpick legs. But he did manage to stay upright. Expecting him to collapse any minute, we kept watching.

Within, I swear, no more than sixty seconds, that baby gazelle went through a transformation that was impossible to believe. He stopped wobbling, started nosing the box, and then tried to climb out! Nancy picked him up to give him some oral medicine and he vigorously butted the syringe.

I suppose gazelles in the wild had better be up and ready to run within minutes after taking their first drink, and this little guy was. In less than an hour he was bouncing off the walls.

Sammy's mother never did accept her baby. Nancy and Dick milked her out one more time but it was so time-consuming for them and traumatic for the mother that they switched little Sammy to goat milk. He never slowed down.

At the time, Nancy and Dick had three other Speke's, two females and a male, plus little Sammy. None of the others understood what Sammy was. According to the zoos that have raised them, baby Speke's gazelles spend all their time sleeping. Not Sammy. He spent it racing around his pen and ricocheting off the walls. He grew twice as fast as do gazelles raised on their mothers.

Sammy became a handsome young gazelle used as a sire to help increase the captive population. As of 1999, Nancy and Dick had seven Speke's gazelles, several raised on goat milk.

While it is great fun to watch small, weak, baby animals grow strong on goat milk, we all know that nothing takes the place of that first milk from a critter's own mother. And so it is rewarding and exciting to be able to milk out a little endangered gazelle enough to give its baby a good start in life.

THE ELUSIVE
NEW BARN

In 1996, I wrote that my new barn was an imminent possibility thanks to mice. As it turned out, that was a premature hope. The new barn has taken a back seat to a carriage house to contain my horse-drawn cart, wagon, and a heated tack room for the harness and saddles. As of 2000, the carriage house is not yet built, but there are posts in the ground. That's better than the goat barn: we're still arguing about where to site it.

Three years ago, though, it seemed as though the mice had pushed the goat barn project forward. Our barn is old. So old not even the oldest old-timers in the area remember when it wasn't here. It's one of those gambrel roof types with loafing shed added on the north and west sides. There's a track at the very top of the loft that was used in the days before bales, when loose hay was pulleyed into the loft. Like I said, this barn is old.

The south walls are pretty much gone. The wood floor has rotted through in places. The roof, on the side we haven't reroofed, leaks. Johnny was filling a water bucket in the south side kidding pen one day when he leaned against a beam — and fell out of the barn. The beam was no longer nailed to the floor below. That's because there is no floor below. It rotted out.

I know I'm making this sound like a pretty sorry goat operation, but, honest, it doesn't look as bad as it sounds. That's because years ago we covered the whole thing in bright new yellow metal. That didn't stop the rot but it made it look better.

There are so many projects on this farm — fixing fence, building more fence, replacing gates, putting in more gates, shoveling manure, plus building the aforementioned carriage house-to-be — that the goat barn project keeps getting shuffled to the back burner. In 1996, it almost got shifted ahead thanks to mice in the milk room.

The milk room has a concrete floor that has shifted as the ground below it and the building above it have shifted. Now there is a large gap between shifts. The metal cabinets in the milk room are rusted. The metal we lined the walls with has separated from the floor. (In case you wonder why we cover everything with metal, Johnny is a metal-roofing contractor.)

All of this shifting and separating means there are lots of places for rodents to enter the milk room. I do not like rodents. I especially do not like the mice that moved into a drawer of my cabinet in the summer of 1996.

I keep a three year planning calendar in that drawer. It's very handy to have three years at a glance. I can tell when I bred which doe to what buck, when I last dewormed, who freshened when with how many kids, what month the nitrogen tank was last refilled, and so on.

I also keep all my farm income on that calendar. When a goat is sold, I write down the amount on the day I sold her. If I disbud or castrate for someone else, the charge goes on the calendar.

In other words, all my farm records are on that calendar. Or were. Until the mice moved in. They didn't write things down; they chewed them up. They decided my calendar would make perfect mouse nest bedding. Most of July 1996 became lining for a mouse nest somewhere, as did half of June and a good slice of May. Other months were nibbled at the edges. Little pieces of calendar were strewn all over the drawer.

So I set traps. And caught two very pregnant mice. Of course, I felt guilty for murdering expectant mothers.

I told Johnny I couldn't stand having the blood of mice on my hands, or traps, so I wanted a rodent-proof milk room.

"It's about time to build a new barn," he agreed. "With a new milk room."

Happy days!

Except nothing is that easy. First we have to decide where to put the new barn, what design to make it, what to make it out of, and how big it should be. We've been discussing those points for the last ten to fifteen years, ever since we decided we needed a new barn.

After walking all over the farm, trying out imaginary barns here and there, we finally came up with a tentative location a bit behind and to one side of the present building. And after many years of sketching barns, asking friends for suggestions and laying out possible floor plans in the pastures, we finally agreed on a tentative floor plan.

For years we'd talked about the next milk room. Would it be up to Grade A standards? Lined with fiberglass? With big picture windows overlooking the pond? I have this vision of fiberglassing all my show ribbons into the walls of the milk room. It seems a shame to have them stored away in the attic where no one can see them.

"Could be," said Johnny.

And what about an observation deck above the milk room? For goat and pond watching?

"It's a possibility," said Johnny. (He never says yes or no. Things are always either "a possibility" or "could be". I think it's a man thing.)

But then the mice moved in and I was not as interested in watch towers or fiberglassed ribbons as I was in tightly sealed doorways and crackless floors. Besides, towers and fancy milk rooms are costly.

We still haven't settled on a definite floor plan or location. The old barn continues to deteriorate. The carriage house is next on the list, then we can save up money for the new barn.

I don't think the mice need worry about losing their old home any time soon.

SUCCESS

"Have a good day," I've discovered, has a dramatically different meaning to a city person than to a goat person. I'm not qualified to say what it means to a city person, but I'm sure it doesn't mean "a day without a goat getting sick, getting out, or getting into trouble."

My friend Sally, a goat person, says, "I consider my day a success if all mammals on the place are fed, not bleeding or in pain, and all are accounted for. I consider it a plus if I don't have to go anywhere (which would entail getting dressed in 'civilized' clothing) and the telemarketers are phoning a different state."

I agree with Sally. Except I would not just consider it a "plus" if all the above criteria were met. I would be ecstatic. My "good day" standards move lower each time some disaster occurs. After one memorable week, a good day became one where I don't have to take goat lungs to the vet clinic.

My vet treats both small and large animals. He usually comes to the farm but this day, I just needed a vet to look at lungs. We'd put down a goat whose lungs had been damaged, we suspected, from pneumonia that I had not discovered and treated soon enough.

I'd already gone through all the guilt of thinking I had not adequately cared for this goat, and the tears before asking Johnny to put her out of her misery. I had at last composed myself for the 25 mile trip to the vet clinic. Stoically, I sat in the waiting room with my grungy bucket concealing goat lungs.

It happened that this morning my vet was out on calls and the other vet, who primarily handles the small animals, had a string of appointments with foofy little cats and dogs that needed examinations because "Widdle sugar woogums Foofy doesn't seem to feel too good today. Does him, Foofy?"

Now I love my animals, too, but there are people who go a little overboard if you ask me.

No one, however, asked me. What they did ask was what was in my bucket.

"Lungs."

"Lungs?"

·"Yes, from a goat that died."

"Oh, I'm sorry. How did she die?"

"We shot her."

Noticing the stunned expression on the gentleman's face, and the way he pulled his sweetie pie kitty cat even closer to his chest, I hastened to explain.

"She had pneumonia and couldn't breathe well."

"Oh."

The conversation sort of lagged after that.

Between this gentleman's appointment and the next appointment was no time for the vet to look at my lungs. (I didn't have an appointment.) The second client had a wire-haired mutt of some sort who smelled my bucket and began growling and hiding under her owner's chair. I tried to move a bit farther away.

The mutt owner looked at me oddly. "My dog is usually very friendly."

"I guess she smells what's in my bucket."

"What's in your bucket?"

As before, the conversation deteriorated from this point on.

The next person in the clinic was a very large man carrying the tiniest dog I've ever seen. It turned out to be a six-week-old Chihuahua, about the size of a newborn goat's head, or slightly smaller. Thankfully, this dog was too sleepy to care about my bucket.

The large owner stuck his little mite of a dog about four inches from my face and said, "Isn't him dust the cootest iddle ting?"

I avowed that him was, although I can't focus on anything that close to my face.

"What's in your bucket?" was his next question. I quickly leaped up and asked the receptionist if I could

just leave my bucket since the vet was apparently too busy to look at my lungs now. Then I gratefully fled without looking at the large man who, at the mention of my bucket's contents, had quit gurgling to his miniature dog and become deathly silent.

If I ever have to take parts of deceased animals to a vet again, I'll go to the back door wearing dark glasses, drop off my parcel and leave.

Most days, fortunately, I don't have either dying or sick goats. If I did, I wouldn't still be raising them. But a healthy goat can disrupt good days, too. She can step in the milk bucket; squeeze through a gate with the herd following; and, of course, the most frequent and favorite activity, poop in her water bucket.

A reasonably good day is when I discover an escape before the goats reach the fruit trees. Or when the feed store actually has in stock the milk filters I forgot I was out of until I tried to strain the milk. Or when the goat spills the milk bucket soon after I start milking instead of waiting until the bucket is completely full.

A city person would probably think that "success" to a goat breeder would be wins in the show ring or selling our goats for big prices. But Sally and I know that success comes in far less grandiose packages.

Are the goats all where they belong? Not sick, not bleeding, not in pain? Are they fed and their buckets poop-less?

If the answers are all "yes," that is success.

DEAR DEPARTEDS

Goats die. All of them. Eventually. That's one of the sad truths of goat raising. Those adorable babies you grow so fond of over the years will eventually grow old, or sick, or both, and die.

I've lost quite a few long-time friends over my many years in goats (30 years as of this writing). I still miss them . . . Deedee, Delilah, Total Eclipse, Hondo, Gigi, Phantom, Spirit . . . the list goes on. These goats are all buried on this farm. Deedee and Delilah were 14 when they died, Gigi 16; Hondo, Total, Phantom and Spirit were 11. When goats stick around that long, you get attached to them.

"Real" farmers, I'm told, don't get sentimental over their animals. When an animal is no longer of service, it's culled. I can cull young animals, but not long-time friends. My goats feed my soul as well as my body. So, okay, I'm sentimental . . . but I'm not alone.

For many years, sentimental friend Kathy and I made a trek in March to the Oregon coast in memory of her foundation sire, Sidney Chinsucker . . . What can I say? He sucked her chin when he was a baby . . . and of my beloved doe, Total Eclipse. (She was born during a total eclipse of the sun.) Total was the first permanent champion American Nubian I ever raised. Sidney and Total both died in March of 1990. Kathy and I cried together.

Sidney, a many-times over champion, was a popular

fixture at Northwest goat shows in the 80's. He and Kathy had a special relationship. Sidney weighed at least 400 pounds, nearly 4 times what Kathy weighed, but he would not have hurt her for the world.

However, he wasn't eager to walk around a show ring, even for Kathy. We in the stands laughed till we cried as Kathy pleaded and tugged while her gentle giant balked and sprayed.

When Sidney died, Kathy had a vet put Cecil down. Cecil, Sid's best friend and long time companion, would have died of loneliness. That's what happened to my Delilah after her twin Deedee died. She quit eating and starved herself to death.

Cecil was a wether and bigger than Sidney. It would have taken a huge hole to bury the friends together. To make things even more difficult, a ferocious storm arrived at the same time Sid and Cecil left this life. Getting equipment in to dig a mammoth hole was out of the question. The alternative was cremation.

Human crematoria do not cremate animals, Kathy learned. So she called the local humane society.

"My two beautiful, wonderful goats have died and I'd like to have them cremated," Kathy said through her tears.

"Why, of course. Bring them in."

Those poor, unsuspecting people. When the humane society heard "goats", I'm sure they were envisioning animals the size of large dogs, not small horses.

Kathy and three big men loaded the deceased goats into a pickup truck. Even under ideal conditions, getting animals that heavy into the back of a pickup would not be easy.

The conditions were anything but ideal. These were not elk that could be cut into hunks before loading. Not with Kathy around. What with the heavens thundering and shooting bolts of lightning and dumping sheets of rain, the straining pallbearers (one of whom was weeping to rival the clouds) had quite a time.

Sidney was not about to make his passing easy, even

after arriving at the crematorium. After an animal is cremated, bones remain. The bones are ground up and added to the ashes. The humane society found out, to its sorrow, that dog and cat bones do not compare with the bones of a 400 pound buck. Sidney broke the grinder.

The poor lady at the humane society called Kathy and apologized for taking so long to give her the remains of her dear departeds, but some of the remains were still bones and it would take days to repair the grinder.

The next time the kind-hearted lady called it was because there were more ashes than could possibly fit in the cute little urns available, the ones they used for dogs and cats. The sweet lady hated to ask, but could Kathy please bring something bigger . . . preferably metal, with tight-fitting lids?

Sid and Cecil were considerably more manageable after cremation and after the grinder was fixed. They eventually came to rest on Kathy's mantel, safely ensconced in the only metal containers with tight lids that Kathy could find — an extra large canister set: flour, sugar, coffee and tea. Well, actually, Sidney, Sidney, Cecil and Cecil.

Total Eclipse doesn't reside in a canister. It wasn't storming when she died. Johnny and I buried her under many feet of dirt and buckets of tears. Those goat folk who have never dealt with the death of a long-time goat friend are missing something. For one thing, a lot of crying. And either a heckuva big hole or a whale of a lot of ashes.

But there's also a sense of closure when you bury the same animal you watched arrive, all wet and full of promise, years before. The doe whose first freshening you awaited with such anticipation, who accompanied you to so many goat shows, who gave you so many offspring and so much milk over the years. And, who became a best friend.

Food for the soul, that's what goats are. And that kind of food nourishes far longer than flour, sugar, coffee and tea.

THE PERFECT ANIMAL

As much as I love my horses and llamas, I must admit they are not as useful as goats. Goats are the perfect homestead animals. Nothing else does so many things so well. My goats provide food, clear brush, fertilize the garden, mulch plants, furnish potting soil, and give me attention when no one else will.

True, I can't ride the goats or spin their wool. However, I could drive them to a cart if I cared to. (Or had the patience to train them.) And we have tanned the occasional goat hide, although never used it for clothing. Nonetheless, the potential is there, as Johnny often reminds me.

"Isn't she pretty?" I ask him, as we admire a colorful yearling.

"Yeah, she'd make a great rug."

I try to keep the fine qualities of goats in mind when I'm doing the daily barn cleaning. Knowing that the manure and straw I'm shoveling will someday be rich, black soil helps make the job less tedious. And when goatlings leap into my wheelbarrow, knocking it over and dumping my morning labors back onto the barn floor, it's nice to have something to threaten them with.

"Get out of my wheelbarrow if you don't wanna be a rug!"

It's the all-purpose quality of goats that makes them so useful to the homesteader. It's their personality that ensures the homesteader will have twice as many goats as needed for food, fertilizer and friendship.

Llamas, I'm told, are as addictive as goats. People acquire more and more of them. But llamas don't provide you with milk. Supposedly, they will guard your goats but we have four llamas and none gives a rip what happens to the goats.

Llamas are beautiful, but only one of ours is friendly, and even he is not as overwhelmingly friendly as the goats. At least, my goats. It's a trial to walk through the barn because every goat wants undivided attention.

Sheep just want to be fed. Likewise, poultry and pigs. My horses are affectionate, but they don't give milk, at least not to me. Neither do the dogs. And dog manure does not make good potting soil.

Nope, there is simply nothing like a goat. This fact may slowly be coming known to the suburban population. I had a phone call from a reporter for the Danville, California, newspaper. Danville, I was told, is about forty miles inland from San Francisco Bay. It is, I gather, a rather affluent community of people more prone to own poodles than goats.

Yet on a walk in the park early one morning, the reporter met two young women each walking a pygmy goat on a leash. The reporter was quite astonished and asked the women all about their unusual (for Danville) companions. The reporter was told what wonderful pets goats make, how affectionate they are, how sociable they are, that you need two of them, and that a very funny book about goats is Life in the Goat Lane. That's how the reporter came to call me. I assured her the women were correct on all counts (especially about the funny book).

I don't suppose suburbia will open its doors to Nubians any time soon, but some of the smaller, quieter breeds may appeal to yuppies who are tired of potbellied pigs, hedgehogs, chinchillas, or whatever is the latest craze.

As I make my daily trips with the wheelbarrow out the back of the barn to the ever-growing manure pile, I think ahead to the next spring, when the mound of straw